REMEMBERING ERNEST HEMINGWAY

REMEMBERING ERNEST HEMINGWAY

James Plath and Frank Simons

[signatures]

Foreword by Lorian Hemingway

The Ketch & Yawl Press

~ Key West ~

The Ketch & Yawl Press
513 Fleming Street, Key West, FL 33040
P.O. Box 6891, Lakeland FL 33807
(888) 715-0723 / e-mail: kwbook@aol

Designed by Tom Corcoran
Cover design by Tom Corcoran and Dinah George
Printed in the United States of America

First Edition, First Printing: May 1999

Library of Congress Cataloging-in-Publication Data
Plath, James
    Remembering Ernest Hemingway / James Plath and Frank Simons
foreword by Lorian Hemingway. -- 1st ed.
        p.   cm.
    A collection of interviews, chiefly of members of the Hemingway
family and friends, about Ernest Hemingway.
    ISBN 0-9641735-5-7 (hb). -- ISBN 0-9641735-6-5 (pb)
    1. Hemingway, Ernest, 1899-1961. 2. Hemingway, Ernest, 1899-
1961--Family. 3. Hemingway, Ernest, 1899-1961--Friends and associates. 4. Authors, American--20th century Biography. 5. Interviews--
United States. I. Simons, Frank, 1939-   . II. Title.
PS3515.E37Z75423   1999
813' .52--dc21   99-27999
                                                                  CIP

For our long (and short) suffering wives,
Zarina Mullan Plath
and
Cyndy Simons

with gratitude for the help
and cooperation we've received from
the people in this book,
whose memories we also
perpetuate.

The authors also would like to thank
Michael Whalton and Carol Shaughnessy
(from the original Hemingway Days Festival in Key West),
Dink Bruce (Key West), Stephen Plotkin,
Allan Goodrich, and James B. Hill (JFK Library),
Marty Peterson (University of Idaho), Allen Josephs and
Susan F. Beegel (Hemingway Society), Christine Pacyk and
Illinois Wesleyan University, Louise Loughlin (Sarasota), and
Ron Anderson (Eau Claire, Wisconsin).

CONTENTS

FOREWORD
by Lorian Hemingway

Ernest Hemingway wrote in his Nobel Prize acceptance speech that "a writer must face eternity or lack of it each day," and if a writer's legacy is to be measured with such exacting calipers then we, as readers, are facing no lack of eternity when it comes to all things Hemingway. The mortality of writers is a given; not so what they leave behind. More fade into obscurity than not, which leaves us with the question of why, of all those who have made their mark in ways both vital and dubious, is not only Hemingway's body of work enduring, but the very essence of Hemingway as well. By the simple testimony of the volumes that have been written about him—biographies, essays, plays (he even appears as a fictional character from time to time)—it is safe to say that despite his passage, Ernest Hemingway, in one form or another, simply will not die. There is reason enough for his endurance. His talent alone, a pioneering form that had its roots in realism, ensures his place in literary history, and because this form was highly effective his work remains both a mainstay and a timely commentary on the very nature of American literature. The often acute sense of irony produced by his spare but oddly elliptical prose well fits the irony of an age in which war and romance were curiously synonymous.

But the simplest reason for his singular immortality lies within the polarity and breadth of the man himself. While making his imprint upon literary territory that still suffered from turn-of-the-century restraints, he at once strengthened and blew away the stereotype of what a writer should be. Never the shy, retiring neurotic man of letters, he lived a life as compelling as his fiction, and became his own best fictional hero. Somewhere along the way the definitive lines between his life and work became indiscernible and the myth of Ernest Hemingway was born. The ill-defined stamp of "macho" was affixed to whatever he produced as a writer and the manner in which he lived his life, and the reading public, accustomed to the comfort of having critics define reality, bought it. In this volume Hemingway's son, Patrick, has some interesting things

Hemingway, shore fishing in Key West, early 1930s.

to say about the harm this lack of delineation between fiction and reality can cause. He asks, does knowing what a strange life Flaubert led give us insights into *Madame Bovary?* He contends, with considerable insight, that this knowledge serves little purpose.

However we view Hemingway, it is necessary to understand that he was, in truth, the first literary figure in 20th-century America who put himself out there for the world to see, and consequently to judge. The fact that he wrote of war and courage and love and loss and seemed to live these themes on his own time made it all the more easy for us to casually erase those once-definitive lines.

My own tie to the man has suffered from this same lack of clarity between fact and fiction, and his influence in my life has been formed, in part, by his writing, and beyond that by nothing more than a series of impressions and a few hard facts. Occasionally I am asked why I often refer to him as "Hemingway" and not "my grandfather," and each time I must examine the question and understand that the answer is, simply, because that is who he is to me— Hemingway, with the myth, the legacy, the lore and the lineage all mixed up, so that the distance between myself and him becomes abundantly clear. I did not know the man. But there are forever three things that come to mind when I think of him.

The first is a memory of his picture on the cover of *Life* magazine that sat on my grandmother Pauline's TV stand in Pine Bluff, Arkansas shortly after he died. Often I would stare at the picture from across the room, trying to gauge the look on his face, the focus of it inward-looking and pained. Some days he looked like an old man about to cry and I would become embarrassed and turn away. Other days he would appear infinitely weary and I would wonder vaguely, the way a child does, what had worn him down. To this day that picture is a testimonial to all I did not know about my grandfather: his life, his work, his last hours, and what had marked his eyes with such defeat. Still, it was an odd comfort to see that picture year after year—my grandmother kept it in the same spot on the TV stand until she died—the color faded from it, the bottom edge curled from where it rested on the stand. I could feel compassion for him, seeing that picture.

The second thing that comes to mind is something his only brother, my great-uncle Les Hemingway, said to me once, strong

Hemingway, with marlin, Bimini, 1935.

words of advice given when I was desperately caught in the process of trying to "know" my grandfather. I was in my 20s then, and as a young woman who had spent an inordinate portion of her life searching for her heroes, that TV-stand picture still a ghostly hall-mark of that heroism, I was looking for a safeguard against my own defeat. I had to know what made Ernest work so that I would not ever make the same mistake and go down like he did. Knowing him in some way, even through words and impressions of others, seemed to offer a tenuous form of both instruction and absolution, and early in my adulthood I imbued him with the characteristics of a saint and, disappointed by news to the contrary, turned to Les to plead for a truer picture of the man. His words to me were: "You can never know what goes on in the mind and heart of another, be he far or near. Even if he writes it down, you can never know, because who says that this is the man unless he tells you so. You can only guess and often it is the guessing and the hoping for what isn't true that gets you in the worst messes. But you can make him anything you want. A bastard. A hero. Just remember this, what I'm about to tell you, and from your respect for me or your lack of it you can go forward with at least something and leave the rest of the garbage behind. But don't ever listen to the muckrakers. They've peered in where they shouldn't have and even then they didn't know what they were seeing. He was a good guy. Simple as that. He was a good brother."

I did respect Les Hemingway, immeasurably, and for a long time his words were enough, and I was able to hold tight to this one-dimensional view of the man as good and nothing less. Still, legends get you where you live, seep into some unconscious strata and grab hold, forcing you to eventually define yourself in relation to another. Once I truly became aware of Hemingway's tie to my own passions—fishing, drinking, writing—I began to believe that there might be nothing I could do to put the brakes on the inevitable. If there was something to the notion of genetic fate, then I was sure-ly doomed. Call it the Granddaughter Theory.

As it turns out, there are no safeguards against defeat, and in my late 30s I had to face down the killing reality of my own alcoholism. Through this I became more familiar with, and even felt I knew to some degree, a truer Hemingway, the man far beyond the bravado who must have lived within the confines of an individual purgatory so consuming it took every ounce of his will to deny it. And when he could not he bore the definite cross of being human, and in that death, defeated though he may have seemed, deserves not reverence, but compassion and respect. Respect for his craft. Compassion for his journey into territory that, despite his talent, despite his personal courage, could not be charted.

It is through his writing, I know now, that I have come to know my grandfather, and not through the myth that merged, into a grotesque form, the celebrity of Hemingway and the hard, raw reality of his writing.

In "The Snows of Kilimanjaro," Hemingway writes of one duty in life to which, it seems, he was honor-bound by an unspoken code within him, a truth in himself unavailable to the curious, that never bore the mark of his celebrity:

"There was so much to write. He had seen the world change; not just the events; although he had seen many of them and had watched the people, but he had seen subtler change and he could remember how the people were different at times. He had been in it and he had watched it and it was his duty to write of it."

In these interviews friends of Ernest Hemingway give us something of the man who was "different at times," a man beyond the narrow window of what he would have had us know, and it is a collection of which scholars should take note because here is the person who emerged when he was not writing; here is, through the eyes of Betty Bruce, Tillie Arnold, Bud Purdy and others, a man who encompassed the dimensions of friendship and instilled in those he left behind an unshakable loyalty. They do not regard Hemingway through the lens of celebrity or myth, and when these notions occasionally arise they steadfastly defend his right to have been, simply, who he was, and through their loyalty we come to understand something of the very private world of Ernest Hemingway. Here are people who witnessed the vulnerability of his last years and who worried for the health and fate of their old friend. They are, for the most part, everyday people. Not intellectuals. Not editors. Not publishers. But mostly friends—people he trusted and who in turn trusted him. They speak here to the truth of that trust, with startling conviction and an abiding affection. Most telling of all, perhaps, is how they manage, with no trouble whatsoever, to separate Hemingway the friend and man from Hemingway the writer. It would not be unwise to take their lead.

Lorian Hemingway
Seattle 1998

REMEMBERING ERNEST HEMINGWAY

CHARLES and LORINE THOMPSON:
A Key West Friendship

His closest friendship was with Charles Thompson, a broad-shouldered, brown-blond young man roughly his own age. Charles loved hunting and fishing with something of Ernest's own passionate devotion. Pauline immediately took to his handsome wife, Lorine.

[Carlos Baker, *Ernest Hemingway: A Life Story*]

In April 1973, I parked my Ford wagon on a narrow shell driveway in Key West and rechecked the address given to me by Charles Thompson the previous evening. The three-story graystone, on expansive corner acreage, appeared empty and isolated in the lush tropical surroundings. There were no visible neighboring houses, and it was far from the traffic so common in this tourist mecca. I stepped through the open gate hinged to a five-foot wall which appeared to surround the property, then walked the long path through the front lawn, up the steps, onto the large concrete-floored porch.

The night before, as soon as I'd arrived on the island and checked into the motel, I had impulsively leafed through the phone book. There he was, *Thompson, Chas.* This had to be Baker's guy, Hemingway's best friend. I rationalized that the worst that could happen was that he'd say no, especially since I'd had no prior contact with him by letter or phone.

I was relieved. His was a kindly, soft-spoken voice, and, in truth, I was surprised when he agreed to meet with me, for I could imagine all the calls he'd had since 1961. In 1969 Carlos Baker had first published a portion of the biography in *The Atlantic Monthly*, then the complete book with Scribner's.

In a corner of the Thompsons' wide porch stood a large elephant tusk, well over six feet, propped heavily against the wall. I recall hoping, as I stood on the porch, that the tusk could be a talisman of my being in the right place at the right time.

Thompson greeted me at the door. Despite my sincere efforts at saying a proper hello, I was torn by the distraction of the large glass-cased gun rack immediately to my left in the foyer. Later,

Thompson would identify the large assortment of guns and match them to trophies taken. I would heft them and, with his encouragement, work the actions and check the sights. Which is the famous 6.5 Mannlicher? The one that Margot used on her unfortunate Francis? Which of these did you use for the kudu? For the water buffalo, the rhino, and the lion? Which of these, did you say, belonged to Hemingway?

I admit to serious excitement, thinking safari and *The Green Hills of Africa.*

Frank Simons: How did you meet Ernest Hemingway?

Charles Thompson: In the spring of '28, Ernest, Waldo Pierce, Mike Strater and Archie MacLeish and I went fishing. [Eddie] Bra Saunders took us in his cruiser to the Tortugas. Georgie Brooks had seen Ernest fishing off one of the bridges—this was before the highway came through and you had to take a ferry halfway—and they got to talking and he told Ernest that he knew somebody who liked to fish. I was working in the hardware store, and Ernest came into the store one afternoon and he introduced himself as Ernest Hemingway, the novelist. I had to laugh, because here this young fellow had come into the store and told me he was a writer, and he was now living in Key West and wanted to do some fishing, and he said that Georgie had sent him to me. I had a little boat, a nineteen-foot, built like a sailboat with an open hull all the way down, with a little engine, and so I took him out after work.

FS: Catch anything?

CT: Luckily, we did hook a few tarpon. I think we did the first night. He was so excited. Archie MacLeish came down later that spring and we fished. [John] Dos Passos and Bill Smith came down. I think that was Ernest's first saltwater experience, I'm not sure. But we had a nice time.

After Ernest came into the store that first time, I came home that afternoon and told Lorine that I met a guy today that claimed he's a writer and he said he was going to need a boat [laughs]. I didn't realize that he had written two books by then. He had just come from Paris and was working on *A Farewell to Arms.* The first time he came through, it was just for a short while, and Pauline went on to St. Louis for when Patrick was born. Now I didn't think we'd ever see

4

them again, but they said they were coming back, and the next year they came and they asked Lorine, my wife, to help them find a house. They came back every year after that, until they bought the Whitehead house and moved here permanently.

FS: What year did you and Hemingway go on safari?

CT: It was in 1933, because we were back home, I'm sure, for the '35 hurricane.

FS: How successful was the hunt?

CT: Oh, with Ernest very good. We got lion and leopard, but we didn't hunt elephant. Ernest didn't want to kill an elephant. I don't know if it was the size of them or what, but we got pictures of them.

Ernest got a nice lion with a golden mane. Here's a good picture [he reaches to a nearby table for a small framed photo of Hemingway and his lion]. The hunters got so that they called it a "picture cat"—that is, we would shoot a zebra for the lions and they would come trottin' out just like you rang the dinner bell for them—and that's how we got that picture. So if it was known that there was a lion nearby, we'd shoot something for them to eat so that the party of tourists could take pictures. Ernest shot that golden one.

FS: I suppose he was pretty excited.

CT: He wasn't too excitable a person. I mean, he got upset sometimes. There were four of us who were supposed to go, Mike Strater, and Archie MacLeish and myself and Ernest, but those two backed down, so Ernest and Pauline and I went. We got to know each other.

FS: You must have enjoyed reading his book, *The Green Hills of Africa.*

CT: I thought it was an interesting book.

FS: I imagine it was pretty amazing to see yourself portrayed as Karl.

At this point, Mr. Thompson pales and shakes his head, asking that the recorder be turned off for a moment. It's fair to say he was visibly upset.

FS: Do you feel that the character, Karl, was an accurate portrayal of you?

CT: No, not at all [He is shaking his head slowly, and whispering.] But I'd rather not say too much about that because, you see, the man's dead.

FS: So it really wasn't that way at all?

CT: The characters were fiction, which is what a novel is about, a made-up story. It was a good description of the country and what it was like to hunt the big game over there.

FS: What of the notion that Hemingway didn't hesitate to use his friends to further his career?

CT: Yes, for writing. But I don't think he'd take advantage of them. When he was writing, I think he was impersonal, you might say. If it was something he wanted to write about, or use a friend as a character that he wanted to put in a book, I don't think he hesitated to do it, whether it made his friend look good or bad or what. I think when he became a writer, anything goes. After all, he was writing fiction.

FS: Do you think he did this in *Green Hills* when he wrote the character Karl?

CT: Well, as I said, I'd rather not go into that, except to say that it was a book of fiction. But we like to talk about Ernest, which we've done quite a bit lately. It comes in streaks, like now. We like to talk about Ernest because we were very fond of him.

FS: And that is the trophy kudu, the one that there was so much contention about in the book?

CT: Yes. I hunted with Ernest's boy, too. The second time I went over with Patrick, who was a white hunter over there. He moved way south at one time, I think, or he may be still up in Nairobi around Tanganyika. Patrick was in Arusha on the Cape-to-Cairo Road at one time. The town of Arush is where he lived, and where he used to hunt on the Serengeti Plain.

Where we hunted in 1933 [Hemingway, Thompson, and Pauline], you go over the Ngorongoro Crater, which is an extinct volcano, and it's cracked broad at the bottom and the grass is grown up—date palm grass in the mud bottom of this extinct crater—and the animals would often graze there.

FS: During those early years, in the late twenties, do you recall his looking to the local color for material for his work?

CT: He was very observant, and he would go down to the docks with the fishermen in Havana and talk to them, and the same way down here. I mean, a lot of his friends were boatmen, like Jakey Key and those people who ran the party boats. When I say "party boat"

Charles Thompson, at his home in Key West, 1973.

I mean those that carried three or four people, I don't mean the big ones that take thirty or forty.

And he was a very good friend of Bra Saunders. In fact, Bra was a friend of mine and he had a little boat we would take out for some fishing. It had a little sail on it, as I told you. Ernest was a very observant man and very kind and would help people—you know, the rummies, those who were down.

FS: So you think of him as a good guy as well as good friend?

CT: Yes, he was a good man. I have some of his books he signed for me, *The Old Man and the Sea* and some others. [Thompson gets up from his chair and reaches to a book shelf, selects several volumes of first editions, and hands them to me.] A lot of them he autographed, but towards the last there, he didn't.

Ernest was a very outgoing man, but very fair too, and he would sit down in a bar and talk, and, you know, he would get stories. He had a very charming personality. I mean, people would talk to him down on the docks, and, of course, he spoke Spanish.

FS: Tell me about the fishing.

CT: There was lots of fishing, up and down the Keys, and down to the Tortugas, and I went over to Cuba with him too, when he first started going over there. But he tried to do things right, he wanted the big fish, the big animal, and over in Havana we went out and we caught some small white marlin, and when we came in he cut one up and gave it away, and the next time we came in the whole dock was just crowded with people, a couple hundred anyway, because they knew we'd have fish. I guess they were poor and hungry. There were one or two guys Ernest was friends with, and so we gave the catch away. Ernest liked to talk to the Spanish people.

FS: Obviously, Cuba became very important to him.

CT: Eventually he moved to Cuba and he lived over there, finally, near a little fishing village called San Francisco de Paula. And he took all of this very seriously, because the fishing was better—larger marlin, very big fish—and I guess he made friends over there too, you know. He liked the boatmen, and he would sit there and talk with the Cubans on the dock.

FS: So he moved to Cuba for the fishing?

CT: He still liked Key West, but it was about that time that they [he drops his voice to a whisper], he and Pauline, were breaking up. I don't know if we should print this, but one reason he went to Cuba, I don't know if Martha went over there because he was there or what, but she had found this place outside of Havana. And when I went over there, after he moved and had a home, I tried to play tennis with them. I had met all his four wives: Hadley, Pauline, Martha and Mary.

Thompson and I turn to echoed footsteps on the hardwood stairs as Mrs. Thompson carefully makes her way down the steep open staircase into the morning's sunlit great-room, and Charles calls to her.

CT: Mama, did Martha come before Mary, or Mary come before Martha?

Lorine Thompson: Mary after Martha [laughs]. Hadley, Pauline, Martha and Mary.

FS: Do you think Mr. Hemingway was more interested in spending time with the local fisherman—whether in Key West, Bimini, or Cuba—instead of writing?

CT: Well, I was just going to say as you speak of him as Mr.

Hemingway, that everybody knew him as just "Ernest." But what I mean is, his friends were the regular people—carpenters, fishermen, working men like J.B. Sullivan, [Sloppy] Joe Russell and Bra Saunders. I mean, he loved to talk to people and would go down to the docks and just sit and talk. Don't you agree with me on that, Mama?

FS: Do you recall his brother, Leicester?

CT: Mama, whatever happened to Ernest's brother, Hank? His brother, Leicester, was kind of heavy set, sort of on Ernest's build. "Hank," we called him. Ernest was about my height, about six-one, maybe a little heavier than me, but not fat.

LT: Hank wanted to be a writer like Ernest, but he didn't have Ernest's charm at all. The last I heard he was running a newspaper somewhere in the Bahamas.

FS: How important was Pauline's family to Hemingway?

LT: I think some of the family money helped him when he got started. Mr. Pfeiffer, that was Pauline's uncle, was the one that financed the first trip to Africa. You see, what happened was when Ernest's first book was a success, Uncle Gus handled a problem for him with Pauline's parents.

FS: Did Hemingway have a problem with Pauline's parents?

CT: Uncle Gus Pfeiffer had said to Ernest, "You're putting all this money to your family. Isn't there something that you want to do?" and he said, "Yes, I'd like to go to Africa," and that came from that.

FS: What do you recall of his children while he was living in Key West?

LT: He had two children by Pauline and one by Hadley. Patrick and Gregory were Pauline's boys, and Bumby—John—was Hadley's. Patrick was a nice boy—they were both nice boys—and Gregory was the youngest. Patrick and Gregory had nicknames and we had known them since they were born. Bumby was Bumby when he came here.

CT: Didn't he always call Patrick "Mice"?

LT: Mouse. And Gregory was Gigi. I don't know why he called Patrick "Mouse." Anyway, he loved his children, and the writer of *Hemingway the Father* had talked to Bumby. A fellow from Chicago telephoned down here and wanted to know what year Evan Shipman was here and tutored Bumby. He came down several winters, and the one winter he tutored Bumby he taught Bumby math by race track things, part of racing [laughs].

FS: Can you speak of Hemingway's interest in racing?

CT: We didn't have much contact with him on the races, but we know that the bullfights were, you know, his thing.

FS: Did he talk much about the bullfights?

LT: Yes, he did when Sidney Franklin was down here. When they got together, Sidney and Ernest would mess with the cape. I don't know whatever became of Sidney. He used to come down quite often.

FS: Do you recall Martha Gellhorn?

LT: When he and Martha went to China—and they didn't like it—before they were divorced, she wrote for *Collier's* and I don't know what he did. But it was about 1941, because I think the divorce was in '42.

FS: As a writer, were things going well for him before the divorce?

LT: When he was running around with Martha? He wasn't writing much fiction. He wasn't very settled during those years. I thought he should spend more time on writing and not so much running around.

FS: Of his books, which do you find the most memorable?

LT: Oh, I don't know. This may sound a bit strange when I say it, but actually I think I liked the bullfight book. I mean, to me, Ernest has more of himself in the bullfight book. Maybe that's why I liked it so much.

FS: Much has been said about Hemingway's lack of female character development in his stories.

LT: Well, I know of his character in *A Farewell to Arms*. She was down in Key West you know. She worked for years down at the library. The nurse that he built the character Catherine Barkley on was a real person.

Agnes was her name, and she was a very admirable person, and when people tried to interview her about Ernest or anything like that, she said that that life was over, and she had nothing to say about it. I don't know if she was here before Ernest came or if she came after him or what. I never did know her personally, but I know that she's not in Key West now. She left a long time ago.

FS: Did you see much of Hemingway after he received the Nobel Prize? I imagine there was quite a celebration.

CT: No, I don't think he celebrated it, did he, Mama? Did he make a fuss over it?

LT: No, those are the sort of things that Ernest didn't get excited about, but, again, I think he was sort of pleased.

FS: What did you think of his acceptance speech, which was read at the ceremony?

LT: He wasn't the sort of person who could make public speeches, never wanted to do them and sort of pooh-poohed them. I never heard him make a public address, but I'm certain he wouldn't have been at his best. He was uncomfortable with the microphone. I think that he felt too often that a person could be misinterpreted or misunderstood.

FS: Do you feel he was misinterpreted or misunderstood?

CT: No two people, or four or five, they see something, and none of them see it the same way or talk of it the same way, and I think it's the same thing with Hemingway. For instance, when I talked to him about something that I might find interesting, someone else might find it altogether different.

LT: Pauline spoke about this when she said that she realized there were a lot of things about Ernest that she didn't admire, but then I think everybody who really knew him had that same feeling. You liked him and were close to him and everything, but there were different traits that maybe different people didn't admire in Hemingway. I thought the world of him.

CT: In other words, there are some exaggerations about Hemingway that you just can't agree with. But the writer Baker spent a lot of time on his book, don't you think so, Honey?

LT: Well, I found Carlos Baker's book interesting, but I didn't agree with him altogether. I think he did a good job—a terrific seven years' work—and, on the whole, you really can't find anything better. You know, he never knew Ernest.

CT: Everybody sees things differently, and all a person can do is make his own interpretation.

LT: I don't know how people can keep writing about him.

CT: One thing about Ernest, if you were interesting, it made no difference to him whether you had money or didn't have money. He was more interested in what you had done and what you hadn't done and what you could help him with. I don't think he would have taken anything from another writer or anything like that. He was very interested in people.

LT: He didn't like phonies, though. I know that was one thing that bothered him. And he could be very nasty with them—you know, sarcastic and everything.

FS: There is an irony here, because some of his critics maintain that he was a phony.

CT: Oh no, Ernest was genuine. He was absolutely genuine. I mean, if he didn't like you, you knew he didn't like you. I guess he got some of his stories that way, when he talked to someone down at the barroom, some poor man as well as a rich man. And of course he had some very fine friends. Alfred Vanderbilt came down here several times and Ernest took him fishing. I mean, Ernest had his friends that stuck with him, and not only that, but some of his friends would be, well, when we're on the barrooms, not what you'd call first class—but then all the same, they were just people to him that he wanted to like, and if he liked you he liked you, and if he didn't, he didn't. And he could see into a person, and most of his characters were genuine. You take *The Old Man and the Sea*, the fisherman was a real genuine character. He just seemed to be able to portray what people were.

FS: Some critics have suggested that he was preoccupied with proving his masculinity.

LT: I don't believe that. There is no truth to that.

CT: In other words, that he did the hunting and all that because he wanted to show that he was brave? But that isn't a fact at all. I mean, to him, shooting a lion and all that was just part of his life, part of what he was doing.

FS: There are those who would say that he loved to kill for the sake of killing.

CT: No, it's the game, the idea of its being a difficult thing to do and you try to accomplish it. It's the same with fishing. You try to catch a big fish because you might lose him, and he might get off before you get him in. A tarpon is apt to jump off as you get him right at the boat. I mean, the number of fish that we caught, we would never kill a fish unless somebody wanted to eat it, or if it was

Hemingway, Bra Saunders, Bill Smith, Key West Docks, mid-1930s.

a man's first tarpon, and we'd bring it in and see to it that we took pictures. But we would release fish all the time, bring him to the boat, release him. Let him go.

FS: You made this point about his not wanting to shoot an elephant, and that dispels that thing about just killing for killing's sake.

CT: Oh, he absolutely did not want to hunt an elephant. He said they were too big and too beautiful. Hadn't you heard him say that, Mama?

LT: Well, that's just the thing that you come up against everywhere, that people just don't understand how anybody can like the sport of killing anything. Most of them don't think of fishing as killing, but shooting an animal is, somehow or other, another thing.

They just don't know what it's all about. They've never done it, so they don't see the challenge.

FS: So it's not about his proving his manhood?

CT: No, no. I mean, any sport you try to do, you do it because it's a little difficult. You try to win at tennis or you try to play golf. Or look better than the other fella.

LT: I think that people don't understand that it's more than a game. It's the challenge. It's so difficult to get, and it's confidence. You're putting yourself against yourself and the game you're hunting. Just as much as if it's tennis, you're competing against the opponent because there is a terrific amount of . . . I'm not a shooter, I can't hit the side of a barn [laughs]. I went out there to Africa, you know, with Charles, but the only thing I ever learned in Swahili, "Show us the way to the big elephant with the long tusks," was as far as I ever got. But I was very excited about Charles getting an elephant.

I liked elephants and all that, but nevertheless, the competition is the thing, I think, that gets you. Now this is from a non-sportsman. I can't shoot or anything else, and I doubt that I'd hit anything, for that matter, but I can see the competition in getting it and how it becomes such a terrific thing.

CT: Ernest got lost over there one time on safari. They just lost track of him over there one time. My, were we upset at that time. When his plane crashed in Africa, we thought he was killed. Of course, it turned out that he lived through the crash.

LT: But I always thought the injuries he got in the crashes may have affected him later, somehow. Because, you see, he'd had so many terrible injuries in his lifetime, and towards the end it seemed to take its toll.

FS: What about Hemingway's critics who argued that he tried too hard?

CT: To show he was a man? No, that's not true. I think he really enjoyed shooting. I liked it, too. Well, we don't have any shooting down here now, but in the old days we used to shoot the white-crown pigeons. Have you seen the white-crown pigeons on the Keys? We used to shoot those years ago, and the thing about them is that in flight they are hard to hit. But they only come here to the Florida Keys, to Cuba, and they go to the British Bahamas and leave in the winter, and then they go to South America. They can shoot them when they go there, but we can't here; it's closed here, all that kind of hunting. But we did in the past.

FS: Did you enjoy reading *Islands in the Stream*?

LT: I read the first part of it. Did it ever come out in book? I thought it was terrible. And the thing I've got against Mary, I don't think she should have let them publish it.

There's this thing about Ernest. He always went over and over and worked on his stuff and I just don't think he had with *Islands in the Stream.* He had an idea or something that might have developed into something or other, but he hadn't finished going over it. But for a thing like that to come out afterwards, I think, was terrible.

FS: Some have said that *Islands* contains a portion of his best work—for example, the fishing chapters, and his description of the little village.

LT: But the thing is, Mary grabbed anything she could get a hold of and published it. I mean, Mary, she just . . . I don't know why she was that way. I remember, some time after Ernest's death, that she came to town, and someone was driving this big car for her, and she drove right down to the bar and collected a lot of Ernest's old papers and things, some unpublished things that he'd left in a back room when he went to Cuba with Martha.

Anyway, I guess there are two schools of thought—one is, if you like anything or everything of Ernest's, it should be published. But, I think too it was financially good for her, because after all, she is in the public eye as Hemingway's wife. No matter what part she played in his life, you're still going to be practical, I guess. But Ernest was fond of Mary. In fact, he was fond of all his wives. And I think Mary was very good for him in his last years, and I'm glad she was able to help him, instead of Pauline, because it would have been very difficult for Pauline, because of the type of person she was, to live with Ernest in his last years.

CT: Yes, I think Mary took good care of him at the end.

LT: Of course, some were finding out that he was getting old and wasn't quite as fascinating or charming, but I think he was.

FS: Was it his depression, his health, that led to his death?

CT: I think when he got so he couldn't do things like he did, when he was young, and things like that . . .

LT: I have never felt so terrible bad about Ernest when he committed suicide, because I think Ernest had an absolute horror of getting so he couldn't write, and he was evidently practically going blind and said he couldn't remember things, and I think he felt it. And I don't think he wanted it to . . . I mean, I think he realized it himself maybe that his writing wasn't what he wanted it to be and he couldn't stand the thought of it. It preyed on him, and he didn't want to get, well, to try to continue writing and have it go into a decline that way.

CT: They had a lovely place in Ketchum, out west in Idaho, where he died. On a little sort of cliff and there was a creek below it, a really lovely spot. He loved it out west. He used to go to the Nordquist ranch out in Wyoming when he first went out there, and he would take Bumby and Patrick and they'd ride horses and hunt with him out there at the ranch.

FS: Was he close to his children?

LT: Yes, I think he was very close to his children. But all of Ernest's life, one thing he always told me, he was always against attaching yourself too much, the same with things and people, and someone once said, I think in a book, that that was cowardly. I don't think it was, but he would never become too close.

They left France because they thought Bumby would become too attached to Pauline there, and he said that to me about my dogs and how I'd become upset when I lost one of them, how people become too attached to them. "They don't live forever," and of course, "Life is short," and if he told me that once, he told me a hundred times. You must not get too attached to things and people in life, you know, because of the disappointment in having to give them up eventually, and therefore, a person has to be more detached. I don't think he was altogether detached, but I think he tried to be detached, and I know with the children he tried to keep them from becoming too attached to him, and I think maybe with his wives he felt the same way about them, and maybe this was a way to remain objective about his writing.

FS: Do you recall, towards the end, that Hemingway became especially suspicious of people?

CT: No, but then we hadn't seen him for about a year before he died. But I didn't mind the book about that at all [A. E. Hotchner's

16

Charles and Lorine Thompson, Key West, 1973.

Papa Hemingway]. There was a part in it where the writer was very good to Ernest, although Mary carried on so much about it. His fear of the law, the revenue people, game wardens, when they went out one morning to shoot or something, the FBI and such. Ernest always had a perfect horror of getting involved with the law.

FS: Was he concerned about following the rules?

CT: Oh yes, he wanted to follow the rules.

LT: I don't know if he wanted to follow the rules so much [laughs], but I know he didn't want to get involved with the law.

CT: Like he didn't want to get caught at it? [big laugh]

LT: Do you remember the night, Charles, that he came over here after a fight with a man, when he and John, they had called the sheriff and were going to have him arrested and he came running over here in the middle of the night? [laughs]

CT: That's when Carl [Charles' brother] was sheriff too, wasn't it?

LT: I think so. Anyway, he wanted you to go down to the sheriff right away. That was a fight that always became sort of a family joke. It was a ridiculous sort of thing. His sister had been down here while he and Charles were in Africa, that was his first trip to Africa, and she brought her child down here and stayed with Patrick and Gregory, and the nurse at the house, and they'd come back [from Africa]. That was Ursula, and she went over to a party at Katrina Johnson's, and there was a man, I think his name was Stevens, or Stevenson, or something like that. I don't know if he was a writer or what he was, but he was there and he made a remark about not liking Ernest's work, and Ursula just got all upset about it and she went home and told Ernest that the man had insulted her. There wasn't anything personal that way or anything, and Ernest just . . .

CT: He misunderstood what she meant, I think.

LT: So he jumped up and went rushing over to Johnson's and was calling the man out and biffed him one and knocked the man over, and Mrs. Johnson, she was very excited, and she came rushing out. She was going to go right in and call the sheriff and Ernest and Ursula came rushing over here late that evening, and they thought he was going to have to go to jail. There was nothing we could do at night, but Charles said he'd go down and see about it in the morning. But it turned out to be nothing. The man came around to Ernest's house on Whitehead and apologized the next day, and Ernest invited him in for a drink [laughs].

I don't know if the man particularly apologized, but if he didn't like Ernest's work, I think it was just Ursula who got excited about it. I don't know what he was or did here, but I don't think he was wealthy or anything. He was a sort of writer, poet or whatnot. He kept wearing a pair of dark glasses for a day or two because of where Ernest hit him in the face.

FS: But there was no lawsuit or anything?

LT: No, nothing really came of it.

FS: Did Mary Hemingway ever sue any writer for anything that they may have said after his death?

LT: The only thing I know of, it was reported that she was going to sue the man that wrote right after his death [Hotchner], but I don't think anything ever came of that either.

FS: Did she have any concerns about the commercialization of his name? For example, Hemingway's Bar, as they call Sloppy Joe's on Duval Street, or Captain Tony's, which Tony Tarracino proudly claims as the original Sloppy Joe's [across Duval on Greene Street].

LT: That could be, but the man is sort of a joke in town. Mary has been very good about such things and has never paid much attention to them. You see, all the time we knew Ernest we never talked to a reporter, and our main concern was, come and get these people out of our house, will you? Keep the people from coming out here. We never gave out any information about him or anything at all. But then Mary came down and told us that Baker was going to do the official biography of Ernest, to feel perfectly free to give him anything, any information, just as we felt about it, because we were really, practically, she said, the only people that could give him much about his life in Key West.

You see, he lived here from '28 and into the forties, and besides the few people who'd come down, like Max Perkins and Dos Passos, Archie MacLeish, and Scott Fitzgerald, he had quite a few friends in Key West, like Georgie Brooks. But I guess we were more intimate with him than anybody else. And so Mary said then, give him all the information, anything you can remember, and any letter or anything we had we should feel free to turn over to Baker. So after Baker published, we were free to talk to anybody.

FS: How does Mary feel about talking to writers and reporters now that Baker has published the biography?

CT: I'm not sure. I don't know where she is now, Lorine, do you?

LT: Well, I have her New York address somewhere, but I don't know if she's still there or not. We used to get a Christmas card, but not for a couple of years now.

FS: After Hemingway's death, how much help or influence was Toby Bruce to Mrs. Hemingway?

LT: Toby probably knew a great deal more about him after he moved to Havana than we did, because when Charles went over to Havana, I never did, because after he and Mary, well, he and Martha first moved to Havana. But after Ernest got the boat, beginning with Martha, and when he went to Cuba, Toby continued to be sort of his right-hand man here doing things for him.

CT: Pauline brought Toby down here from the little town of Pauline's father who lived in Piggott [Arkansas] on big acreage, and

Toby had done carpentry work for them, and she brought Toby down here when she was fixing the house.

LT: Yes, and Toby had made the barn over as a studio and had done a very good job of it. So Pauline brought him down here. It was sort of hard times and things, with the Depression, and he helped her in working with the house and then afterwards he stayed on. After they came back from Africa and Ernest had the boat, he sort of looked after that.

You see, we were awfully close to Pauline, too. And I don't think either Charles or I took sides, but we were hurt when the break-up came, don't you see, terribly. Now Toby was very friendly with Martha. He was here during the Martha period. I don't think Ernest particularly used him at it, but he was a sort of go-between whenever Ernest had to deal with something before the divorce, when he first went to Cuba.

FS: Can you tell me your reaction to Hemingway's death?

CT: [Whispers] I knew him up until he died, and that came as a shocker. I went to his funeral out west in Idaho. Of course, it was Hollywood movie cameras and news photographers, and everything, and boy I got 'em furious, because there was a line, and I was the last in the line and the camera was up here [he gestures over his shoulder] and I turned my back on it [smiles] and it didn't make me very popular.

I'd known Ernest since he first walked into my store back in '28, and we remained good friends up until his death. We had fished the Keys, Bimini, and Cuba, hunted the Serengeti Plain in Africa, and birds and big game out in Idaho and Wyoming. I'll always remember him as my good friend. He won the Nobel Prize, but for me he was my hunting and fishing friend, and we had some good times.

Frank Simons

BETTY BRUCE:
"He was Just a Great Guy"

Betty Bruce had known Ernest Hemingway since she was ten years old—from 1928 until his death. But her friendship with him evolved largely because of her husband, Otto "Toby" Bruce, who also began his association with Hemingway when the author moved to Key West in 1928. Toby Bruce continued to work for Hemingway after he moved to Cuba and then onto Ketchum, Idaho. Bruce chauffeured Hemingway on his trips west to Wyoming, Utah, and Idaho, and Hemingway also depended upon Bruce's skills for the maintenance of the *Pilar* and for repairs at the house on Whitehead Street.

I had called Toby in April 1973, hoping for an interview, but he was tied up with a fire sale at his appliance store and suggested I speak to his wife at the Key West Library. Betty was the librarian, and during our discussion she experienced the spontaneous recollection of what she called "an unbelievable story" which occurred early in 1961 while she was doing research at the library. Betty described her surprise at learning the identity of then-librarian Mrs. Stanfield, who had expressed her concern about "Ernie" because of a wire-service report that he had suffered a heart attack. Betty was aware that only those who knew Hemingway during the First World War called him "Ernie." Subsequently, Mrs. Stanfield modestly acknowledged that she was Ernie's Agnes.

Agnes von Kurowsky, born in 1892, was raised in Washington, D.C., where she worked in the Public Library until 1914, when she entered Nurses' Training School, Bellevue Hospital. During World War I, after having been wounded, Hemingway spent time convalescing in a Milan, Italy hospital. The night duty nurse during his recovery was Agnes, who became Hemingway's fiancée and later the model for Catherine Barkley in Hemingway's World War I novel, *A Farewell to Arms.*

Agnes had lived in Key West for a number of years as Mrs. Stanfield, her married name. Thrilled by this discovery, Betty Bruce told how she couldn't wait to call Hemingway, but was shaken and angered by his reaction. Today, the day of the interview, April 11,

1973, her feelings have mellowed to an affectionate, "The bum!"

Frank Simons: Do you recall Mary's return to Key West after Hemingway's death, and the recovery of stored papers and manuscripts?

Betty Bruce: We didn't really have anything to do with what she decided to keep, the manuscripts and so forth, from whatever she found at Sloppy Joe's Bar, and we didn't question what she found. But we worked with her and I would go through things and anything that I saw that I felt was something that she'd be interested in, why, I would turn over to her. I wouldn't read the letters. I mean, if I would see where or who it came from, or if there was anyone I knew, then I would put all family on one side and any possibility of anyone being of importance, and separate that which I thought was just ordinary stuff, and then she'd go through it, according to how much time she had.

Toby, of course, had worked with Ernest for so many years, but his being in business at the time [he owned an appliance store], he couldn't stay down at the building while we were going through the stuff as much as I did. But again, as I say, it was a such a mess. I mean, things had been there since '38, and this was in January of 1962. There were rats and mice, roaches and everything, and dampness and it all had been just dumped in there. Ernest left, thinking he'd come back some time to go through it, but he never did. Occasionally, he'd ask Toby to get something in particular that he wanted.

FS: What motivated Hemingway to store it there?

BB: Well, Ernest never threw anything away. Everything that was Ernest's, after he and Pauline separated, he had stored in a back room of the bar. Anything that was his. And of course, he took a great deal of stuff with him to Cuba. But these things were a little bit of everything—personal letters, magazines, laundry slips—and he would keep them clipped together, all the various things. There were even lunch tickets, or bus tickets, or railroad tickets. Toby's theory is that he used these as memory checks, to help him recall what he had done during the course of the day. He'd have the grocery lists of what he'd be carrying on the boat, and all these things would be clipped together, I guess, for detail. I don't know, but it's almost impossible to imagine all the things that were there. Collections of old bullfighting magazines, literary magazines, books, newspapers, letters—anything that he was interested in, he kept it. Seven box loads, I guess, and these were refrigerator box loads of stuff, were hauled away to the dump and burned.

It was Mary's wish that everything of no value or importance be burned. This would prevent it from going into the hands of people who were just scrounging. And she really didn't have a chance to go through it all that carefully, though she was here over a month, and she worked every single day from nine o'clock in the morning 'til five in the afternoon in that place, but it was just too much to handle all of it, you know. So she sent back to Ketchum what she considered the important things. During this period, of course, she was staying here in Key West in order to complete this business.

FS: Was it the present Sloppy Joe's on Duval?

BB: Yes, Sloppy Joe's where it is today, only it was in back of the building, and then in the back of that, where the old city hall is, there was a wooden building that backed right up against the Sloppy Joe's building, with just a little tiny alley-way, but it was the back room of that. An old wooden building.

FS: Visitors to Key West can find it confusing that both Sloppy Joe's and Captain Tony's claim to be Hemingway's Bar.

BB: Well, that was because Joe Russell moved his bar. He was the owner of Sloppy Joe's and was Ernest's friend. When Ernest first met him, he was operating a bar in the other building, where Captain Tony's is now, on Greene Street. And then he moved. But during the course of the time that Ernest and Joe were friends, both bars were open, and Ernest would go to either of them. He didn't call the other place [the old location] Sloppy Joe's. I can't remember exactly, but there were two or three different names that cropped up. The Silver Slipper was a little dance hall there. I forget exactly what they called the bar, but it was referred to as Josie Grunts' Bar, because Joe's nickname was not "Sloppy," it was "Josie Grunts."

FS: Is Captain Tony somehow associated with Hemingway?

BB: No, Captain Tony didn't come here until Ernest was long gone. As far as I know, Ernest never went in the bar after it became Captain Tony's.

FS: Did Hemingway have a business interest in the bar?

BB: I don't think Ernest ever invested in a bar, as far as we ever heard. Some may have suggested that, but Joe didn't need money. Ernest might have done it if Joe needed a loan, but Joe was all right. I mean, he had his money. But I know if Joe would have needed it, then he'd have lent it to him. Ernest was generous. But he didn't want to be taken.

FS: Was he taken?

BB: Oh, sure [laughs]. Anybody who would lend money is going to be taken somewhere along the line, particularly someone like Ernest, being a writer and well known.

FS: How do you suppose Hemingway, Joe Russell and their friends spent their time? No doubt they had some drinks, but how else might they pass the time?

BB: Well, he enjoyed gambling, but he wasn't a heavy gambler, not an everyday gambler or anything like that. He liked the races in France and he liked to go to jai-alai, but he wasn't one of these compulsive gamblers, just to gamble. And I never thought of him as a particularly heavy drinker.

FS: During these years, was he on good terms with the city fathers, or with the local sheriff?

BB: Ernest was a writer, of course, and most people came to know that. But everyone, I think, thought well of him and welcomed him during those years. As far as I know he was always on good terms with everybody.

I think a lot of people have confused Hemingway's own life with his books. For example, in *To Have and Have Not*, the characters are in trouble with the law, but as far as I know, that's just a novel. And *To Have and Have Not*, I don't know everything about it, but I believe it is mostly fiction. I don't think it was based on any particular real events, and I don't believe Ernest necessarily had the experiences of the characters in that book, other than, of course, his familiarity with boats and the sea and so on.

FS: Other than what you've already mentioned, what was included in the collection of manuscripts that Mary recovered from the storage room of Sloppy Joe's?

BB: Well, I know there were portions of some manuscripts that Mary apparently took back with her. We found original drafts of some of Ernest's early short stories, and an early draft of *A Farewell*

Hemingway, Toby Bruce, Betty Bruce, Idaho, October, 1958.

to Arms. There were also galley proofs for *Death in the Afternoon* where Ernest had written corrections.

FS: Were there any portions of what came to be a memoir, *A Moveable Feast?*

BB: Of course, the book *A Moveable Feast* is an accumulation of various things that happened much earlier in his life and then was published after his death. But as far as I know he didn't use any of the material that was here for that book, because he'd never asked for any of it to be sent over to him in Cuba.

During the last years of his life most of his unfinished writing must have been with some things that he had over there, memoirs or diary sorts of things. I know that he was working on his big book then [*Islands in the Stream*] and that, I think, was in the bank in Cuba, probably. It was his last fictional effort, I think—what he called his "big book." And yet I understood his big book was not completed.

FS: Did you find *Islands in the Stream* enjoyable?

BB: I read just the one story, the Bimini bit, and I wasn't happy with it. It just didn't sound right. I mean it didn't sound like Ernest, his earlier fiction. I'm sorry, [laughs] but it almost sounds as if someone else finished it so it could bc published. I mean, it sounds as if someone tried to imitate him, but it didn't work, at least not for me.

FS: Did you ever speak to Mary about its publication?

BB: No, but then I haven't even talked to Mary about it and probably would never talk to her about it.

FS: How do you feel about it personally?

BB: It was a disappointment to me that it was published at all, because it doesn't reflect well on his earlier work. If he'd had anything to say about it, and certainly if he'd been twenty years younger, he would have never allowed it to be published. I think, if he'd had the chance, he'd have gone over it until he felt it was good enough.

Maybe this is what he was doing until he became so ill. He was in ill health and we didn't know who his secretaries were, or who was typing and going over his work with him. That can sometimes, you know, be very difficult. I mean, to have a good secretary. Some secretaries think a lot of themselves. I remember a couple . . . [laughs].

FS: You remember Hemingway's secretaries?

BB: Yes, and they wanted to protect Mr. Hemingway from people, and I remember Mary raising the devil with them and saying, "For heaven's sakes, if he can't see people, know people, and be with people, how is he supposed to write about people?" The one I'm thinking of was a young gal, and she didn't really know any better. She was going to mother Mr. Hemingway [laughter].

FS: Do you recall her name? Could her name have been Valerie?

BB: [Smiles] I'm not sure. Possibly, yes, it could have been.

FS: Were you of any further help to Mary after the recovery of the manuscripts from Sloppy Joe's?

BB: Well, this was a very difficult time for Mary, and she asked Toby and me to go to Bimini with her. Ernest had some property there, some land that Mary had to settle some business about. So we went with her to give her a sort of moral support, I guess you'd say. And then she went back to Ketchum.

FS: What about "Papa" Hemingway? What do you know of that nickname?

BB: I don't know. There's a lot of stories about it. Toby says that he recalls that they used to call him "Pop." I wasn't around during this period. I mean, I knew Ernest since I was ten years old, but, of course, I didn't really get to know him until after Toby and I were married. Toby said it was a sort of thing between him and Pauline about, well, "Poor Mama," and "Poor Old Papa," and again, "Poor Old Mama"—you know, like somebody would be saying "tough luck" or something. It was a turn-off, you know, for somebody who was down in the dumps or something, like "Poor Old Papa" [laughs]. Anyway, that's one of the versions. I really don't know of any others.

FS: Do you recall his reference to Pauline in *The Green Hills of Africa*?

BB: Yes, I know that Pauline was supposedly P.O.M., for "Poor Old Mama" [laughs]. I don't recall much of the book because it came out in the thirties, and I was pretty young, so I didn't pay much attention to it.

FS: What did you think of the Lillian Ross interview? ["Profile," *The New Yorker,* May, 1950]

BB: I read it. And then it was finally published in a book form. But I think it's the greatest burlesque that Ernest ever acted. A beautiful burlesque, and completely: "Hemingway claims," "Papa Hemingway . . . famous writer." It was totally tongue-in-cheek. It had to be. It was just Papa having fun, and it was fun to read it. He used to do things about, well, he would play a God-hopper. Boy, he could preach a God-hopper sermon that you wouldn't believe. I mean, it was hysterical, very funny. And I think that in the interview by this Ross woman, he was just having fun.

FS: Do you think that Lillian Ross was naive?

BB: I don't think she was naive, I think that she was just gullible. I think, in the first place, that he was just doing a favor for her by agreeing to talk to her, and then he just had some fun with it. There was another [article], I think it was *The New Yorker* that did that one too, that they did after they published *Across the River and Into the Trees*. That was burlesqued too, but it was Hemingway being satirized by another writer. I think it was maybe a follow-up of the Ross interview [E.B. White, "Across the Street and into the Grill," *The New Yorker*, October, 1950].

FS: Of course, Hemingway expected *Across the River and Into the Trees* to be taken quite seriously.

BB: Oh, definitely, I'm sure he was very serious about it. In fact, I think it was an important book, and I think Ernest was very hurt about it. And I think he got some terribly bad deals with it. We were in Cuba when a wire came through from New York, *Time* magazine, and they had a series of questions and he cabled back a series of answers. They published his answers as if there were no questions and as if he was just babbling. And it was a filthy, lousy thing to do because it made him sound like he was a nut. And he had been pretty flip and pretty annoyed with the questions, and they didn't publish that they were answers to a large series of questions, out of context.

FS: Were they suggesting anything beyond the poor reviews for the book? Suggesting anything about his state of mind, his health?

BB: Yes, they tried to suggest that he was just a babbling brook. Senile. I'll be honest with you, we were upset when we were over there, about a week or so, and Ernest was depressed at times, and we got to worrying about it between ourselves. We were staying at the house.

We were the happiest people in the world when the book was published, because we realized what Ernest had been doing. He was using us as a sounding board. There would be pages of his writing that he was speaking, acting out, using us as a sounding board, you see, to see what our reaction would be, for he was a stickler for actual language. So it was a great relief when we found out that this actually was the book he was trying out on us.

I think that his depression was a reflection of his first feeling of age, the frustrations of age. I think it is a very common and very important phase in the history of his writing development. That's my personal opinion. I'm no critic or literary person. It's just that I feel so much has been misinterpreted. I'm afraid that people who had met Ernest for just a few hours, or something like that, would be completely confused, because the man, during the course of a day, could be five or six different people. He'd move into one mood and maybe into another personality, and that's imagination. You wouldn't say, if you'd been with him for just one afternoon, that you knew the man at all, because he might not be that man the next afternoon.

FS: Your recollection brings to mind that many remain curious about Hemingway the man. Do you think of Carlos Baker's biography as the definitive biography?

BB: It will never be. Never be, unfortunately. Baker is a very kind man and a very hard worker and certainly an excellent writer, critic, and scholar. But he unfortunately never knew Ernest at all.

Ernest had many friends with many different qualities themselves, and from many different walks of life. Certainly he treated some differently than he did others—not because he liked them better, but because there was, again, another challenge, one of personality that he reacted to. He definitely would react to people in his own field with more difficulty. I mean, he had a different reaction to other writers and critics than to his friends.

FS: Why do you think that's so?

BB: It's been suggested that it had to do with a sense of competition. I don't know, but I don't think so. I just know that he wanted as little to do with professors and critics as possible. As for other writers and novelists, I really don't know how he felt about that.

FS: Do you think it was a concern for him that he hadn't attended a university?

BB: No, not really. I think he was quite proud of his really quite extensive knowledge that was self-taught. I don't think it necessarily alienated him from literary circles. I really can't express it. I'm not sure how to say it, but I know that among his friends that were of other professions or occupations, other fields of interest than writing, that he seemed more relaxed, perhaps because it was more relaxing to be with them. He was far gentler and more giving.

I'm sure that there were a certain kind of people of the writing field that he got along well with. But I think that when it came to discussions and things of that nature and things of that field, why, he was more inclined probably to be a little more difficult.

I think a good example would be what Hotchner talks about in *Papa Hemingway*, when Hotchner was assigned by some magazine, I don't recall exactly which one, to get Hemingway to write an essay about literature [*Cosmopolitan* wanted him to write an essay on the future of literature]. And at the time, Ernest chose to write a short story instead.

I think the best book that I have read on what I'm speaking of is *High on the Wild*, by Lloyd Arnold, who was just a photographer friend and who knew Ernest quite well, knew him as a very close friend during the period when he first went out west to Sun Valley. Of course, much of the book is the wonderful photography which Arnold explains throughout the book. But more than that, he explains the whole thing of how they knew each other and the people that they knew in Sun Valley when it was new, and it's quite well written by someone who wasn't really a writer, because it gives a good description, really, of what kind of person Ernest was, his love of nature and so forth.

The book was never promoted. Actually, it was published in 1969, and I understand that Arnold published it himself. [Mrs. Bruce shows me a copy of Arnold's book.]

FS: Why would he have to publish it himself? I agree, the photography is superb. Are you in here?

BB: No, thank goodness. [Laughs] But Toby's in there. Actually, I didn't get out to Sun Valley during the early years. Ernest always promised me a trip, but we did make a trip to Wyoming. I forget when Toby and I went. I guess it was in 1958. But *High on the Wild* was after the Hotchner thing and the lawsuits and whatnot, and Mary wouldn't, for some reason, even though they'd been very close friends all these years, she wouldn't give him permission for publication. She was upset about Hotchner's book, so none of the publishers would touch it.

FS: What in particular was she disillusioned with in Hotchner's book?

BB: I really have never discussed it with Mary, because she hasn't been back but once since the time she was here to pick up the rest of Ernest's things. We occasionally hear from her through correspondence and telephone calls, but, as a matter of fact, we didn't even hear from her at Christmas this year.

FS: Is she still upset with things?

BB: I imagine she is because she's had many, many difficult times, as everyone will, but particularly because of the circumstances of Ernest's death. She said something about coming down this winter. She still loves to go fishing, I guess, but she pretty well tramps the world these days [laughs].

FS: So she's no longer willing to talk to biographers and writers about Hemingway?

BB: I have absolutely no idea. At this point, because of publishing conflicts, I don't really know how she's dealing with that. I've known of cases where she did allow an interview. It probably depends entirely on what the circumstances in her life are. Of course, I imagine she's, well, not bored by it, but I know we are. I'm just so sick of the sound of my own voice on the subject [laughs]. Truthfully, it isn't as if it's an intended imposition nor an intended unfriendliness, it's just purely a matter of simply talking the thing over and over. We've had people from all over the world come to Key West, you know, and it isn't that we're holding back or anything, or not willing to be open with it. It's just that you get, well . . . [big sigh followed by laughter].

FS: Mrs. Thompson also wanted to know why people want to keep talking about it.

BB: Mrs. Thompson is a delightful person. She was one of our first hippies, but don't say that out loud [laughter]. She had strong features, and was very pretty. She wore sandals, and her hair . . . well, she was completely herself, and her strength was in her personality. I've never known anyone who didn't like her. She was Pauline's closest friend, and I think there was always a slight resentment when Ernest left Pauline. But they never showed it to him when he came back, because they always had dinner together, and Ernest would spend just as much time as he could with them.

FS: Did you meet Martha?

BB: I never met Martha. Toby met her, but I know that when they were together, Ernest wasn't too happy about that marriage. Toby never met Hadley. That was the one that he used to always regret not meeting. He's talked to her on the phone many times, when Ernest was taking the children places and one and the other, and picking up the kids—you know, making contact.

Ernest always thought beautifully of her. He always spoke highly of his first wife, Bumby's mother. Anything he had to say was just very complimentary.

FS: Did he ever speak of his break-up with Hadley?

BB: Well, that was very personal. It wasn't the kind of thing we would expect him to discuss with us. I've never been able to ask questions myself. So I listen with half an ear or two [laughs]. I believe those things are personal, and when you're with your friends, they will tell you what they want.

FS: Did you think of him as a physical person?

BB: Oh, definitely. Mainly physical, because I was always fascinated by the fact that whenever he'd enter a room, no matter if it was a pitch-black bar with guys watching television, they would instinctively turn. They didn't know why they'd turned, they hadn't seen him, but they could feel his presence.

Toby's favorite story is when we were headed out to Idaho. Mary and I had flown to Chicago and Ernest and Toby picked us up. He and Mary were going hunting, and he'd invited Toby and me to go with them. He promised me he was going to take me west to hunt sometime, because I'd always been gung-ho about fishing. I'd never hunted, but I'd always loved guns and shooting and target practice. Anyway we stopped in Sheridan, and Toby went to get some ice and a bottle of wine for lunch. The World Series was on, so Ernest said he'd sit in the car listening to the game, and Mary and I stayed with him in the car. A few minutes afterwards, Ernest got the itchkins, so he went in to see if there was a bottle of "Pinch," I guess, because he was always collecting "Pinch" whiskey bottles because it was still rather scarce, so if he could buy a spare bottle in a bar, he would always pick it up, you know?

So a group of men were all sitting down at the end of the bar, and it was dark. Toby said he walked in and this one guy turned around

Gregorio Fuentes, Hemingway's captain on the *Pilar*.

and said, "Who the hell do you think you are, Ernest Hemingway?" And then they all did a double-take. So then he sat down and the guy insisted on buying Ernest a beer or a drink. Sometimes, these aren't very nice people. I mean, my God, if . . . you know, there could have been a problem.

Ernest had had a situation in Bimini. He had just come in from fishing or something like that, and he clobbered a guy. I think he broke his jaw, if I'm not mistaken. It happened on the docks. There was an old guy, a colored man, and when Mary and Toby and I went over, Mary wanted to hear this man's song, because Papa always used to sing it. They called it "Big Fat Slob in the Harbor." I guess a man, a tourist or someone, decided he would call Ernest a big, fat slob. So Ernest hit him. After that, this colored fellow made a calypso of it, and so Ernest used to sing it, "The Big Fat Slob in the Harbor" [laughs].

FS: So he had a sense of humor?

BB: Oh, he had a beautiful sense of humor. And he was a very funny man. He loved a good joke. Loved a good time. Loved music, all kinds. Spanish music, jazz, loved good thirties and forties music.

FS: Did you hear Hemingway speak of Scott Fitzgerald?

BB: I gather that he must have been fond of him, and other times not, but the only thing I know about their knowing each other was what I read. I never met Fitzgerald. Toby says he was here once, but never saw him. I know that they corresponded after Ernest went to Cuba. I knew that Fitzgerald was in bad shape then, financially and emotionally. Toby met Fitzgerald's daughter, Scottie, out in Sun Valley, but Toby never met Fitzgerald.

Our conversations with Ernest were just people conversations. They normally weren't about literary figures or anything like that. When we visited, he talked about things we were interested in and mutual interests of mutual friends. But I do remember that Sinclair Lewis was here, and he went up to the house on Whitehead, and I regretted that on that day I decided not to go swimming with them. Toby had invited me to come and I just didn't go . . . I had something to do, couldn't get loose or something.

FS: You admired Lewis?

BB: As a writer, yes. I enjoyed some of his books, but I've never been a great fan of his. Just the reading, you know.

FS: Did Hemingway speak of Faulkner or of his work?

BB: Well, I know from reading that some have suggested they had a problem with each other. What little I've ever heard on that subject was when Toby and Ernest were making a trip one time coming back from Arkansas. Ernest had planned to stop off and see Faulkner. So from what I gathered, Ernest would have liked very much to meet him. I don't think they ever met, but I think he'd hoped to meet him. I don't know what the reason was that they didn't stop, whether it was weather-wise or time-wise or something, but he had planned on it, and he regretted he didn't get to meet him.

I didn't know Dos Passos well, but I did meet him, and I must say I found him very rude. I remember the time that Ernest shot himself in the leg, when he was trying to shake off the shark and they'd had to come back early from fishing. We were having dinner with Dr. Warren and his daughter, and so Ernest came in and then Dr. Warren had to take him to the office to remove the bullet. And I remember Dos Passos coming in and walking around the dinner table and not speaking or anything, just sort of looking the situation over, and I thought, what a rude man.

There were others, of course, like Archie MacLeish, Mike Strater, but during the thirties, I was really too young to know them. As I said, I was ten years old when Ernest first came to Key West to spend the winter here, and he and Pauline lived across the street from us. That was the year that Patrick was a baby. So that was '28 and the winter of '29. I remember I was about to turn ten because Bumby was five years old, and he had come from Paris where he was living with his mother and had come for a visit. So then there was a long period when I went off to school. And Ernest left Key West in '38.

FS: Which of Hemingway's writing stands out in your mind, perhaps as the most enjoyable or appealing? What about *A Farewell to Arms*, for example?

BB: Yes, I enjoyed that book, and it's curious that you should mention it. This is sort of an unbelievable story. When the word came through that Ernest had had a heart attack in Spain a number of years back, we called Mary and found out that it was just a newspaper report. The next day I happened to go to the library. I wasn't working here then, just doing some research. And the librarian and some other people were here, and I heard this lady say, "I heard that Mr. Hemingway had a heart attack. Can you tell me, is it serious, do you know?" And I said, "Oh no, it isn't, thank heavens, it's all right," because you see, he hadn't really had an attack, and Mary had said he was okay.

But the Swedish newspapers put it out, and they picked it up in this country and we called Mary and she said, "No, everything's okay." This was the last trip he made to Spain, a trip he made to write an Ordoñez bullfight article for *Life* magazine.

Anyway, so as I was leaving, this very nice librarian that we had here, who was from out of town and I didn't know her well at all, Mrs. Stanfield, as I was going she said, "Well, gee, I'm awfully glad to know that Ernie is all right." And that sort of went, *boing!*

The next time I was in I said, "You know, I was curious, did you just accidentally say 'Ernie,' when you meant 'Ernest'?" and she said, "No." And I said, "Pardon me, but you know, only people that knew Ernest early ever called him Ernie. Did you know him?" I asked. And she said, "Oh yes, I knew him years and years ago." So I said, "Oh?" and, "Excuse me, but where was it that you knew him?" And she said, "Well, I knew him in the First World War." I said, "You couldn't have possibly known him in Italy, could you? Were you one of his nurses?" And she whispered softly, "Yes, I was." And I said, "You couldn't possibly be *the* nurse? Agnes?" And she said, "Well, yes, I am."

And it was Agnes von Kurowsky, the gal that he first fell in love with, and you know, it's a funny thing. Ernest, a number of years back, when he was going to have [Mark] Hellinger do his biography, he called Toby and said, "Toby, go down and see if you can find my World War photo album." And so Toby went down and couldn't find it.

So later, when I again saw Mrs. Stanfield, I told her that Ernest had never been able to find his World War I pictures, and I asked her if by chance she had any of Ernest during that period, because I knew that they were missing. She said, "Yes, I do." And I said, "Would it be possible for me to copy them and send them to Ernest?" And she said, "Well, I'd be delighted. As a matter of fact, he can have them," she said, "because, after all, I have no children or anyone, so I'd be delighted for him to have the pictures." So she was Agnes, who was Catherine in *A Farewell to Arms,* and the nurse that Ernest had fallen in love with.

FS: Do you think that she followed him to Key West?

BB: Well, she'd been living here for a number of years and never contacted him once. He never knew she was here. She knew, at the time, that he was in Cuba and that he'd lived in Key West, and she knew when he came through Key West, but she never contacted him.

When they broke up, ending their engagement, he never forgave her. And I couldn't believe this. You see, she broke it up after Ernest had come back from Italy. She was too old for him, she said. She said, "I couldn't have married a man who was that young," because she was twenty-six and Ernest was only nineteen.

Before she returned to America, she'd become engaged to an Italian, but she never married him. She did marry an Italian later, but not the one that she became engaged to after the break-up. But Ernest never forgave her.

So I was kind of thrilled you see, and so I called Ernest and said, here, I found her, and I've got your pictures and whatnot. All he said was, "Send them to Scribner's." And then he said, "She can go to hell!" I was so mad, I thought, why you bum! I mean, she was so nice about giving him the pictures, and he didn't want to see them, didn't want to know about her, didn't even ask about her.

So she, then, even later here in Key West, was apparently very fond of him, but she said she just couldn't see how it could have worked, because he was too young.

He was working on *Farewell* here in '28 and '29, and Pauline had already had Patrick. And that was the first Caesarean when she went on to St. Louis and had Patrick. You see, she was from Arkansas and went to school there and whatnot. Anyway, three of his wives were from St. Louis. And of course, his first newspaper job was near there [*Kansas City Star*]. But he met Hadley in Chicago, Pauline in Paris, and he met Martha here in Key West.

FS: There remains a lot of controversy surrounding Heming-way's death.

BB: It took me a very long time to believe it was suicide. Toby, oddly enough, didn't feel that way. I don't know why I say "oddly enough." Toby knew him better by far. And Toby said, "Listen, Ernest had said to me more than once that he would never allow himself to become a vegetable." But it was still awfully hard to believe.

FS: Did you attend the funeral?

BB: No, they called from Ketchum, and Toby was out fishing and I got the call in the morning—Sunday morning, I think. Anyway, Toby was fishing and whoever called, I didn't know the person. They said, "Papa's gone," and I first went, "Well, where did he go? Back to the hospital, or what?"

He had just arrived, you see, back from the Mayo Clinic, and Toby had wanted to call him that night. And I said, "Oh, don't call him, Toby, because he'll be awfully tired," and so Toby said, "Well, maybe that's a good idea. I'm going fishing tomorrow. Maybe we'll have some good news when I get back."

So when Toby came in, I said, "Toby, the bad word is here. He killed himself." The man who called, I think he was the man who had the motel there that Toby knew [Chuck Atkinson, who owned a restaurant and grocery in Ketchum] and was good friends with Ernest and Mary, and he said that "Ernest had just ached with misery, but now he was free, he'd accidentally shot himself." But accidentally, I couldn't believe. For some reason, I couldn't bring myself to believe it. Now, when he had the plane accident, Toby and I were the first to doubt [that he'd been killed]. We said, ahh, that's a bunch of baloney. He'll be all right, he'll be back [laughs]. Don't worry. And of course, when he then read his own obituaries, he had great fun.

FS: Why weren't you worried about the reported plane crashes?

BB: Well, you see, Ernest sort of had nine lives. For us, his plane may have crashed, but we just couldn't believe the news stories because they had so often exaggerated stories before about him. But he was always interested in death and always interested in . . . well, I guess everybody would want to know how others would react to their death and what they'd have to say, even though it's most likely all written up long before a person dies.

Anyway, that's that. I'm sorry, but I don't feel so bad about it now. I didn't realize he was as bad off as he was, but then toward the end we had not seen him for about a year.

FS: But you knew of the treatment he'd been receiving?

BB: Yes, Toby was terribly upset with the shock treatments, which he'd evidently received for depression, and then the strict diet they'd put him on, and they'd taken something like seventy pounds off him. We knew he'd had a weight problem in his older years, but that was such a terrible shock to take that much weight off him. Toby was awfully upset about it.

He'd been so badly hurt in the plane crash, which was really terrible, and he had had so many injuries to his head—I think they counted twelve, at one time. I do think that the pressures of so many medical things were what really put him under and caused his depression. He didn't want to be a vegetable.

No one would want to live under those circumstances, if their health wasn't going to be any better than his was. There would be no desire to live anyway, especially if you were ill, unless a person had a real fear of death, and I don't think Ernest had any fear of death. That wasn't one of his problems at all.

Anyway, Toby was very close to Ernest, as we all were. I don't think Toby and he ever had a cross word. I got mad once [laughs]. Toby never got mad.

FS: What made you mad?

BB: Well, it was a reflection on Toby's judgment or something, which I think Toby took perfectly all right, knowing that Ernest misunderstood what the situation was. When I saw Ernest I told him that Toby would not do anything that would not be in his best interest, and Ernest laughed and didn't care enough about the situation to want to know the circumstances. But I was uptight about it, so I said so [laughs]. There was a big ha-rumph, but nothing beyond that.

But Toby and Ernest always had a good relationship. Pauline always called Toby "Otto," because that was his real name, and "Toby," his nickname. It wasn't until after Toby and I were married that Ernest started calling him "Toby." So all of these earlier years he always called him "Otto," like Pauline. And in fact, Mary called him "Otto" for a long time. Then after the war, when we saw more of Ernest, he caught the habit of "Toby," from me.

FS: And now it's been over a decade since his death. So how do you feel about everything, the whole experience of you and Toby and Hemingway?

BB: I think that we have had the most marvelous luck, Toby and I, and most Key Westers have had the most marvelous luck in meeting accidentally and getting an opportunity to know so very many interesting people without having to be anybody but ourselves, without having to be anybody. We've had an awful lot of good experiences. And I certainly think that whoever had an opportunity to know Ernest and be around him enjoyed his friendship, because he was a marvelous character. Very likable. He had a great capacity for life. He was just a great guy, there's no doubt about that. Toby and I will always miss Ernest.

Frank Simons

BILL GEISER:
All Talked Out

Bill Geiser came to Key West in the first few months of 1959, when Ernest Hemingway was no longer living on the island. But as an employee of Charles and Lorine Thompson, he found himself preparing and serving food at dinners for a number of writers—including frequent visitors Ernest and Mary Hemingway. Though the celebrated novelist died in 1961, Geiser said that the quest for information about Hemingway in Key West has been unending. During the twenty-seven years that he worked for the Thompsons, he has talked to a steady stream of journalists, teachers, and professors—and avoided or turned away just as many.

When I first phoned Geiser to ask for an interview, he said he had nothing more to say, he'd said it all over the past twenty-seven years. "What more can anyone possibly say about Hemingway that hasn't been said before?" I don't know, I told him, but every year at least five new books and dozens of articles are published on Hemingway. We'll never know if there's anything left to be said unless we talk. "All right," he said, "I'll be out on the porch this evening if you want to stop by."

When I arrived that evening, July 22, 1998, at Geiser's hair-styling establishment, The Carriage Trade, at 529 Eaton Street, he told the locals he was chatting with that he had to talk to another journalist, and made a face as he did so. Yet, after he asked them to leave their seats to give us some time alone, he eagerly shared letters from Pauline Pfeiffer Hemingway to his employer, Lorine, as well as an oil pastel of Ernest as a bullfighter that was drawn and signed by one of the matadors whom Ernest had assiduously followed. "I'm going to get this framed," he said. Geiser, a vigorous man who resembles actor J.C. Flippen, also produced a number of other eclectic Hemingway items, including baby announcements and photos of the trophies shot by Charles Thompson and Hemingway in Africa on safari. "I thought you might find this stuff interesting," he said. "Now what was it you wanted to know?"

James Plath: What were the circumstances of your contact with

Hemingway?

Bill Geiser: I was working for Charles and Lorine Thompson, and they were the ones who hunted with Ernest Hemingway and traveled all over with Pauline . . . and the other wives. And what I feel, I never hear anybody mention Uncle Gus, and Uncle Gus was the one who put up the money for the boat and the house down here. And I never hear anybody mention Uncle Gus.

JP: The biographers mention him.

BG: Do they? I never hear anything about him, and it's a shame, you know. See, I only got here in '59, so I only knew Hemingway for the last year or year and a half. And I feel—and Lorine and I always talked about it too—he evidently knew what was wrong with him and he wasn't going to suffer, and I think that's why he went out there [to Ketchum, Idaho] to do what he did. But Charles was so very fond of him. He would sit, years after Ernest was dead and gone, and gloat about how they would be out in Africa hunting and he would always have the best trophies—and that would really kind of upset Ernest. You've seen them at the Thompson property, haven't you?

JP: Yeah. And I understand the trophies are for sale now.

BG: They're gonna sell them? God, I could have had them all. I didn't want any part of them. I didn't even want the one where the elephant had only one tusk. Anyway, where was I?

JP: You were working for the Thompsons, and Ernest Hemingway would come over to the house.

BG: Ernest would come over every afternoon and they would drink and eat dinner, shoot the breeze, and talk huntin' all the time, and I didn't pay much attention to it. I'd be scurryin' around gettin' dinner ready and what have you. And it would take them forever to eat, 'cause there was always drinkin' and "haw-haw" laughin' and all that, you know.

JP: Were the Thompsons also big drinkers?

BG: Oh, yes. With Charles, beer. Mama, she liked gin.

JP: And Ernest?

BG: I don't know. Somethin' in a bottle. The liquor was always set out, and they helped themselves. I'd do the food and see that Charles was all right, see that he gets to bed, pay the bills, go shopping, take care of them when they were sick, all that kind of stuff.

JP: So you did the kind of things that Toby Bruce would have done for the Hemingways.

BG: Yeah. But Mama never liked Toby Bruce, I don't know why. He used to do the nicest things for her. I guess he talked so much about Ernest, maybe that's what upset her. After Ernest died, he acted like he knew everything, and she said, "He doesn't know as much as he thinks he does."

Mama Thompson, she was very fond of Pauline, and when he mentioned his other wives she would be upset about it, because Pauline was the only wife that . . . and she got discouraged with Ernest because he never put in enough time with his children. They needed a father, and he just was too busy to bother with them. Mama Thompson used to talk about how she had to take them up to Miami for treatment all the time. And you know, they never really visited much in my years. I only remember Patrick one time coming over there. I do remember getting phone calls, and I would explain the condition of Charles. But she was always upset about Ernest not taking care of the boys properly, and that upset Charles too. He was very fond of Ernest, but he shared that feeling with her because they really liked the boys and they never had any children of their own. Charles tried to come in and be a father image to the boys when Ernest was gone. Charles loved to fish, and Charles had a couple boats, and over on the bight over there they'd put off in little sailboats. I remember Mama saying one time, "Ernest would like the kids to be hunters, but they're not interested in killing."

JP: And yet Patrick and Gregory became white hunters in Africa.

BG: They did, but according to Mama they never had that interest when they were boys.

Mary wasn't too friendly with the Thompsons, because she knew that Mrs. Thompson and Pauline were very good friends. But it was still cordial, and there was still lots of laughter when they came to the house.

JP: Earlier you were telling me that Hemingway had a number of favorite expressions.

BG: Oh, yeah, he had a lot of off-color sayings. Mama Thompson used to always use that one. We'd be out riding, and she'd say, just as Ernest would say, "Ahh, stick it up your ass, a good thing will never hurt you!" [laughs]. Oh, we used to use that phrase all the time. Charles used to die laughing at him. And Charles' mother couldn't stand him. "Oh," she'd say, "here comes that drunk again." She couldn't take it.

JP: And yet, Lorine said that Ernest didn't drink that much.

BG: [Raises eyebrows, rolls eyes]. Well, at the end I don't think he drank as much. But he was quite a drinker. A woman who worked as a maid at the house there for years with them—she's dead and gone now—she told me that back in the thirties they would hold the dinner until eight, nine, ten o'clock at night waiting for him to come home from Sloppy Joe's, the oldest one [now Captain Tony's]. But you know, he didn't spend an awful lot of time here [in Key West]. He was more or less over at the Isle of Pines in Cuba, his favorite spot. I used to go over there with Mama Thompson and Charles to the Ambos Mundos Hotel, that's where he stayed at a lot, and we would go there for the weekend. I made three trips there with them. We'd fly out on Q Airlines, and the plane was over there in a few minutes. We'd go to the hotel and then we'd meet the Hemingways later on. Then we'd go to the Bodeguita [del Medio]. Now, I never saw any money transactions. I don't know how it was done. I don't know whether they billed us because they knew us, or what. But we ate up on the rooftop at the Ambos Mundos and they would fix birds for us—which I don't like—little birds that they shot.

JP: They just restored the Ambos Mundos, and turned Hemingway's room into a museum.

BG: Did they? It was a very simple room, you know. It had a very plain bathroom where you pulled the chain, and a little bird cage… it had two iron beds in there, and there were no windows, just shutters that opened. That little bird cage was fascinating, that elevator.

JP: Was Hemingway different in Cuba than here in Key West?

BG: Oh, yes. Everybody loved him in Cuba. And in Spain too, they were really fond of him.

JP: What was it like when you would visit him in Cuba?

BG: Everybody just flocked around him, they enjoyed him so much. We'd just come walkin' in there and everybody would announce who he was, I guess. I can remember Dorothy Kilgallin, she was there one day, and she threw her arms around Ernest, she was so excited she got to meet Ernest.

JP: Could you describe a typical night on the town in Havana?

44

BG: Very quiet, when you think about it, sittin' around drinkin'. And he had a lot of people with him that had fished with him and they would come and chit-chat and talk to him.

JP: What topics would come up? Cuba at the time was under Batista's rule, but it was a time of transition.

BG: They didn't talk politics, I can tell you that. I can remember, Ernest was kind of upset because we wouldn't go out to where he was at [the Finca Vigía, his home in Cuba]. I was very unhappy there. What I didn't like about it, we'd go out on the streets and these military patrolmen were walking around with guns, and they were kind of nasty to us. And that's why I was glad when we got back on the plane to come back to Key West. This was the end of Batista's reign, and Castro was takin' over and all that.

JP: So did you not talk politics because it just wasn't done?

BG: We didn't talk about Batista or Castro at all, because you didn't know . . . Mama wanted to see the waterworks, we were not very far from where the pump station was, and they were just as nasty to us as possible when we went there. We just turned around and just kind of walked away from them. I didn't want to get involved with them in any way there, because even at the airport they were very hostile. They took us all and put us in a glass room and there were a lot of people leaving there with chickens, plants, and all kinds of stuff. They were gettin' the hell out of town. A private plane would roll up and boy they would load this stuff up. People were leaving—the money people were gettin' the hell out of there, because they knew what was goin' on and we didn't. So we got back here and a few weeks later I thought, God, I wouldn't have gone over there had I known. We thought [Castro] was gonna be great, but we didn't talk about it.

JP: Did you walk to the Bodeguita, or were you afraid of the military stopping you?

BG: Oh, yeah, we walked. They were just around, even after Castro took over. They were lurking. I always felt that someone was listening over our shoulders. We went up to the old Morro Castle, and oh, my God, it was awful, there were so many prisoners down in there. The guide who was with us said, "All that yelling, that's the prisoners down there." I couldn't wait till I got out of there.

JP: The feeling is different now. In December 1995, I was invited by the Ministry of Culture to deliver two lectures on Hemingway at the Finca, and we were free to walk anywhere in Havana and no one gave us a glance. We were surprised that we could photograph anything we wanted, and we never saw any armed police. They had walkie-talkies, and that was it. The writers we talked to said that they fought censorship in the seventies and won, that, except for journalists who wrote for the state newspaper, *Granma,* they were all free to write whatever they wanted. Some of the time we spent talking with artists and writers, and the rest of the time we spent wandering around Old Havana.

BG: Some of those old buildings on those old avenues are beautiful, but they've just gone to hell.

JP: Were you, or was Charles Thompson, in Cuba during that famous fishing tournament named for Hemingway—where Hemingway and Castro met for the first time and were photographed together? Since Castro won that tournament, I'd love to find someone who was there who could talk more about what happened.

BG: I don't remember anything like that.

JP: Was there any talk about that tournament during your dinners with Ernest?

BG: No.

JP: At the Bodeguita or anywhere where there was conversation, did Ernest take center stage, did he sit back and observe, or was there give and take? What were the dynamics of a conversation in which Ernest was a participant?

BG: They talked an awful lot about their trips, which wouldn't interest me at all—things that would happen to them on safaris—and then they would laugh. I can still hear Ernest saying, "Lorine, I'm always amazed when I see you still around after how you used to take off barefooted over there [in Africa]." And she said she had enough dog on her, the smell of it, that no animal would track her. But she was always barefooted, she loved that, and he would always make that remark.

I think that Ernest was realizing that he was being accepted as somebody. For many years Mama Thompson said that he doesn't realize that some day he will be a well-known writer for what he's writing. But for years she said that she didn't think he realized how well-known he would become.

JP: Did talk of Hemingway's novels or short stories ever come up?

BG: No, I only remember him, one time out at the house . . . some lady here [Valerie Danby-Smith Hemingway] used to type his work and all that, and he used to talk about how great she was. He thought the world and all of her. And Mama Thompson talked about it with him. I didn't know what they were talking about, but she had already read what he was writing from the original script.

JP: He'd show Lorine Thompson his work in progress?

BG: Oh, yeah, he liked to show Lorine. She was a teacher, you know, and he'd show her what he'd written and she'd say something like "I don't think this part sounds so good," and she'd make little comments here and there.

JP: What was it like in Key West when Ernest came for a visit?

BG: See, I'm busy, I'm doin' my thing, and they're around on the side porch doin' their thing, and I'm not paying too much attention to them.

JP: This is at the Thompson home?

BG: Right, at the Thompson house on 1413 South Street. I don't remember where the Hemingways stayed when they were in Key West, but that's where they got together. That's where the heads and the guns were.

JP: What was Hemingway's demeanor that you witnessed on a day-to-day basis?

BG: I guess an ordinary person. Like you're sitting here, you look like something he would have looked like.

JP: But was he engaging, abrasive . . . both?

BG: [Pauses] Okay, I wouldn't pick him as a friend. It wouldn't be for me.

JP: Too flamboyant?

BG: I don't like people who drink a lot.

JP: Then he was still drinking plenty in 1959.

BG: Sure, they were drinking. He'd come there at suppertime and in the early evening they'd have their drinks and all. The Thompsons were great people, and they loved to entertain. Anytime you could take people home there, Isabel always had enough food to feed everybody. And you didn't have to call, "I'm bringin' two or three extra," because she always had somethin' extra, she always had somethin' cooked to add to whatever it was. We had a lot of writers who'd come here all the time, and they'd annoy the hell out of me. Just like now. I don't like this.

JP: The biographers seem to agree that Ernest also preferred the company of everyday people to writers.

BG: I can remember one time when Charles, he was at the gate over at the house, and some man came up and said that he was a writer with some magazine or newspaper or something like that, and Charles just said, "Well, just a minute while I go get the gun, because I wanna shoot you—I don't want to see another writer." And that man ran like hell.

JP: What year was this?

BG: Well after Ernest died. In his later years, Charles would get confused. His mind started to go, and his eyesight was going too. That's why I stopped people from going to the house. They would try to ask him questions about Ernest and all that, and half the time he didn't even know who he was talkin' about. So I just stopped people from coming to the house. Same way, Mama, she got to the point she didn't want to see anybody. People would come and I'd say, "I'm sorry, we're going out riding," which we did. She had two dogs, and we rode for hours and hours, every day.

JP: It must be tiring, but he's as culturally significant as Marilyn Monroe, Elvis, or James Dean, and that means the interest will probably never wane.

BG: This place here [529 Eaton Street] is where Pauline and Lorine had their shop, and the doors were always open. And there was every hunting magazine available on the table in the waiting area. This was a place for men to hang out, not women. This was the decorating shop. Pauline called it The Caroline Shop; Pauline Hemingway and Mama Thompson ran it. They made the drapes and everything for the ships and quarters. All the contracts that they would do for the military bases were with men, not women in those days, and this was a hangout place. Right after I took over the building [the Thompsons gave him the property around 1965], they still would come. Writers, trying to find out information. And that's years after everything.

James Plath

PATRICK HEMINGWAY:
"...a Picasso, a Braque, a Miró..."

Ernest Hemingway's second son, Patrick, was born in 1928 to Pauline Pfeiffer after a long, protracted labor which is generally regarded as the model for the climactic Caesarean birth scene in *A Farewell To Arms* (1929). Patrick Hemingway grew up in the house in Key West where the family lived off and on for roughly ten years, and later spent most of his adult life working in Africa. Now retired, he lives in Montana. The interview below was conducted on May 29, 1986, and was first published in *Clockwatch Review* III:2 in conjunction with the 1986 Hemingway Days Festival. Patrick, though talkative, was reluctant to share specific anecdotes about his father, saying he was going to use that material himself some day.

James Plath: John Updike, in reviewing *Islands in the Stream*, commented that "Hemingway speaks across the Sixties as strangely as a medieval saint." Ernest Hemingway is a hot item again, but is he locked into our literary history, or does he still have something to say in the eighties?

Patrick Hemingway: No writer who is of any permanent value doesn't continue to speak through time. I think we're a little bit preoccupied with our particular time, whether it happens to be the eighties, or the sixties, or the twenties. I would just say that he speaks to any generation, any time.

JP: What, exactly? How would you describe it?

PH: I would say that he has the same thing to say that other artists of his generation—not necessarily writers, but especially painters—had to say. I feel that he is a modern artist, in the sense of a Picasso, a Braque, a Miro . . . that is, those people who began to take reality as something in itself, about which you tried to avoid any secondary adornments: just the primary impression of reality. And this is called modern art, but in painting it was already in existence before World War I, and pretty nearly over by the late thirties.

JP: How much of that can be attributed to his time spent in Paris?

PH: I think it had a lot to do with it, in that his early friendship with Gertrude Stein allowed him to meet, really, the best painters of his time . . . and to meet them when they weren't as generally known as they were later.

JP: How would you explain your father's line where Nick Adams says, "I want to write the way that Cézanne painted?" Critics have tried to tackle the quote, but I think they've all come up empty.

PH: Well, it's a hard thing to do because it is modern art, used in that very limited sense . . . art that they couldn't stand later on in the Soviet Union, and which is valued so highly everywhere else.

I think he also wanted to paint like Gris. Have you seen *The Garden of Eden?* The jacket on that is a Gris painting. He owned two paintings by Juan Gris: one, the matador which was used as the frontispiece in the original hardcover edition of *Death in the Afternoon,* and the other was called *Man with a Guitar,* and that's a painting that always hung in his bedroom, wherever he lived.

JP: And all this relates to the way he and artists of his time saw reality?

PH: Not reality so much in the sense of the impression, but a simplification, something that would create the emotion of a visual reality.

JP: That's what he meant by wanting to write as Cézanne painted?

PH: Yes. Or like Gris, or Braque.

JP: In the light of your brother Jack's new book, I believe that makes you the only member of the estate, the direct heirs, who has not written a biography.

PH: I have to straighten you out there. None of Hemingway's children were heirs. His will left all of his property to his widow, who was stepmother to all of his children. So what Hemingway's children have is the right to share in the renewal copyright . . . but none of us are heirs, and there is no estate, except perhaps for Mary Hemingway and her property. It is a disinheriting will.

JP: How do you feel about that?

PH: Well, at the time I was sort of puzzled by it, but now I think that he had his reasons, and I don't resent it . . . but I don't like to be called an heir when I wasn't. I'm just a son, just a child.

JP: Why haven't you written a biography? Both of your brothers have written one, and Mary has written one.

PH: I think that I would very likely write something, but I have

Pauline, Gregory, Ernest, Jack, and Patrick, Bimini, 1935.
Combined weight of four marlin on rod and reel: 1,552 pounds.

felt that what was outstanding about Hemingway as a writer was that he was a writer of fiction . . . and until I can feel myself able to write fiction, then I'd just as soon not write. I'm not particularly interested in memoir, except perhaps for my own daughter. But I feel that my younger brother Gregory wrote a very good biography of my father. Have you ever read that?

JP: Yes. I thought it was quite similar to some of the others... especially the Hotchner. They covered much of the same territory.

PH: Is it simply similar to Hotchner because they moved in on us? I think that Hotchner is an exploiter of celebrities. Didn't he do something on Doris Day? And now he's closely associated with the actor, Paul Newman? I mean, if there's a resemblance between Hotchner and my brother, it's because Hotchner took over what belonged, really, to my brother, by making himself a surrogate son of Ernest Hemingway and capitalizing on it to his personal profit.

JP: Motivation aside, how would you rate the biographies that are out now on your father? Which one would you say best captures the truth, in spirit and in fact?

PH: None of them. They're all very poor. He hasn't yet had a really good biographer.

JP: That includes Carlos Baker?

PH: Well, Baker's biography is the one I would recommend. I think it is a good piece of scholarly work, but the way it's put together, it is essentially a scanning of Hemingway's correspondence. And therefore, aside from the tremendous amount of effort of assembling all the sources, there is very little input. It is, in other words, a summary or a paraphrase of Hemingway as he revealed himself in his letters. You could program a computer to do the same . . . but it is a good piece of scholarly work. I think that, to a certain extent, is what the scholarly life is, isn't it? I mean, one shouldn't intrude too much of one's own personality, but I think when you come to write a biography of a personality like Hemingway's—which was very powerful and enigmatic—then it requires a great deal of scholarly ability . . . and I'm not so sure that Carlos Baker has that.

JP: Can a good biography of such an enigmatic figure be written without collaboration with the source?

PH: As the dust settles and there's more insight into what Hemingway was trying to do as an artist, I think that there will be a good biography . . . but not in this generation of biographers, because they are generally in a hurry. They're trying to profit.

JP: Pressured or enticed by publishing houses?

PH: I think every major publisher would like to bring out a biography of Hemingway, because it's guaranteed to sell a few copies.

JP: There's a strange controversy now surrounding *The Garden of Eden,* where people are lining up for or against its publication.

PH: Yes, there does seem to be a bipolar reaction to it.

JP: I don't want to get into whether the book should or should not have been released, because I think you've made it publicly clear that you approve. What I would like is your response to the approach editor Tom Jenks used as "storyteller" instead of critic.

PH: Well, I think his approach is essentially the same one that my father would have had to use. If he would have submitted the manuscript Jenks had to work with—1500 pages—then cut down to a printed 270, or whatever, he would have been forced to do essentially the same thing.

Criticism, I always feel, is a distinctly different activity from creative writing. You get in trouble when you start referring to green as blue, and so forth. And someone who is cutting a novel which is too diffuse, too long, or too whatever—that it won't hold the reader's interest—that person is not acting as a critic, he's acting as an editor. My father was always his own editor in that sense. He never allowed Max Perkins to be his editor as he was for the first Tom Wolfe (we now have two Tom Wolfe's, so we have to distinguish between them). But the author of *Look Homeward, Angel* was a prolific writer of just thousands and thousands of pages. It was always necessary for them to be cut, you know? That Hemingway is now being edited by Jenks is certainly something that would never have happened in his lifetime. You can't get around the fact that when someone dies and their work is unfinished, it can never be finished. I mean, you have to remember this is a posthumous work. He himself would have undoubtedly done something to it, but what he would have done we will never know.

JP: There's a letter that your father wrote to *Little Review* editor Jane Heap which, I think, might prove your point. It's not dated, but since it seems to have been written when he was in Europe, that would place it in the twenties . . .

PH: Right . . . early in his career. And what does he say?

JP: He says, "Listen Jane, while I appreciate your delicacy in keeping me out of such attractive company in the magazine, was it because that piece you asked me to write wasn't considered good enough? Because when you think something is rotten, don't hesitate to say so. Then I would read it over and see whether it was or not, and if it was, fix it or destroy it, and if it wasn't, tell you to go to hell and publish it somewhere else . . . only for Christ's sake, don't be delicate."

That, to me, indicates what you just implied: that Hemingway was confident of his critical and editorial ability, even early in his career, and also, perhaps, that *The Garden of Eden*, if it wasn't destroyed, was something he considered salvageable.

PH: Yes. People forget so quickly. Not a single reviewer has made reference to the posthumous work of F. Scott Fitzgerald. What about *The Last Tycoon?* I mean, that wasn't in shape for publication either. As I remember, it was Bunny Wilson who put that together. So this is nothing new. Why don't they compare it to *The Last Tycoon?* Did Jenks do as good a job as Wilson? You have to ask yourself, will the reading public, and especially the reading public where Hemingway is a part of their reading life, be disappointed or not to see a work that he was working on? I think that it will receive a much wider reading, say, than if all the manuscripts were printed in holographic, photographic form in some obscure scholarly journal.

JP: Of the memories that you personally have of your father, are there any which stand out as being totally different from the Hemingway you read about?

PH: I suppose there are, but . . .

JP: You don't carry them around in your billfold?

PH: [Laughs] Unless I get down and put them on paper, it looks as if they'll be lost to humanity. I mean, I really like the idea of writing something about my father, but if I would do so, again, I would write it as fiction . . . which is not to say that certain aspects of the people could not be readily identified. But I think this is true of almost all writers. A good example was Mailer's novel, *An American Dream.* Surely when you read that, there are some people that you can recognize, but they are not called by their names, you know? And they are changed. Anybody who writes fiction improves on reality. That's what that crack of Oscar Wilde's meant: nature is always copying art.

JP: Your brother Gregory is a doctor, Jack seems to have embraced the Hollywood lifestyle, and you're out there in what New Yorkers would consider the wilderness. It seems that each of the sons has branched out into one of the aspects of the father.

PH: Yes, that's certainly true. When it comes to following in the footsteps of your parents, I think that people either react strongly for, or strongly against. The aspect of my father that intrigued me the most was his trips to, and love for, Africa. I lived from the time I was twenty-one until I was forty-seven in East Africa, where I was a professional hunter and taught in schools for game wardens and professional hunters. I was a white hunter in Africa and a teacher of white hunting in Africa for at least twenty-five years . . . and that's a very clear-cut career. I mean, if you ever want to know anything about how to hunt buffalo, or elephant, or rhino, I can tell you how

Detail: Pauline and Ernest with three boys, Bimini, 1935.

to go about it. I was a member of the East Africa Professional Hunters Association, I was a member of the committee of the Tanzania government for licensing hunters, and I was a forestry officer in the agricultural organization of the United Nations.

JP: The hunting and warfare as topics, I think, has provided fuel for people who try to pigeon-hole Hemingway's writing as being "macho."

PH: Well, the whole term "macho" is taken from another culture—the Spanish-speaking, Latino culture. People either like it or they don't like it, but it's very different from the Anglo culture, you know? Was he therefore more like a Spanish man than an American man? I think the answer was yes, because he spent much of his life in Cuba and in Spain. He's on record as saying that Spain is the country that he loved the most. And I suppose the other country that he loved was Michigan, you know? That's the thing he wrote about the most. He did not like Oak Park . . . never said anything about it at all. He wrote quite a bit about Cuba, and about Key West.

They were closely intertwined, you know, being only ninety miles apart.

But he believed very strongly in his destiny as a writer. One of the things that's very true about all this is that Hemingway is as great a writer as Picasso is a painter. And because of that fact, it's very hard to reduce him to ordinary terms.

JP: Was it a burden, having a father so mythologized in his time?

PH: He was a very good father. His family life and so forth he handled quite easily. That is not as difficult to do as to be an outstanding artist . . . which he was. I think once you move into that category of talent, almost everything about you as a person in every other respect becomes fairly insignificant. We don't know very much about Shakespeare, and it doesn't seem to affect the issue at all. I mean, an artist is there in the work that he did . . . and whether he was a father, or anything else, it becomes quite irrelevant.

JP: Is there too much written about Hemingway?

PH: I think that there's a lot said, and it's undoubtedly very interesting. There's a lot said about Flaubert, but what emerges about Flaubert was that he lived all his life with his mother, and that he was a bit strange. But it doesn't help us understand or appreciate *Madame Bovary* one bit. *Madame Bovary* stands on its own two feet. No matter how much we know or don't know about Flaubert, it really doesn't make any difference, because *Madame Bovary* is much more alive and well than Flaubert. Just as I think *Hamlet* is a lot more alive and well than old Will [laughs]. He stares out of a rather bad, you know, steel engraving—or whatever it is—that you see in the bars.

JP: Speaking of bars, Key West was a fairly rough bar town in the thirties when you were growing up there, wasn't it?

PH: Well, I never got too much insight into that, because I was just too young. Most of the times when my father went in for a drink—"a quick one" as he called it—I would just stay in the car. In those days we had a Ford, a Model A, and I remember [laughs] sometimes it would be a long wait.

JP: You mentioned if you did write something, it would be a fiction. Are there any characters or incidents from your Key West or Africa days that stand out as being possible prototypes?

56

PH: Yes, I am very interested in the period when my father was in Africa for the last time, in the fifties . . . when he had the two crashes. I think that his trip to Africa and what happened there is extremely significant in his life, as was the last time that he went to Spain.

JP: Significant in what way?

PH: That's still my business.

JP: Are there any clear candidates for your fictional protagonist or antagonist?

PH: Well, fiction is something very different in that you use your personal experience, but you also use a lot of other things: your reading, your knowledge of how these things are put together, and so forth. When someone paints a picture, it has to be done on canvas in one dimension, with the limited palette that's available. So the conventions of writing fiction change everything. If I may say so, I abhor reality. A story that is real definitely diminishes it in my eyes, because I don't know what reality is. I'm not smart enough to know.

JP: You've mentioned painting quite often in our discussion. Do you paint?

PH: Yes, I started out wanting to be a painter. It was what I did at first, but going to Africa really coincided with my stopping painting. I got very much caught up in a life of action in Africa, and that life of action stopped my artistic life.

JP: Did you ever get to meet any influential painters as a result of having a famous father?

PH: Yes. One painter that I met who had an early influence on my childhood was a very close friend of my father's, Waldo Pierce. But he was never too much affected by modern art. His painting was more Renoiresque. And he did a very fine portrait of my father which has not been reproduced very often. It belongs to my stepmother, Mary, and it's a picture of him during the Key West period.

JP: Any desire to go back to an artistic life now?

PH: I have gone back to it. I'm doing some writing now, and writing was an art that never interested me when I was young . . . it was always painting. But now I feel that writing interests me more.

JP: Is there anything about Hemingway, finally, that you've been wanting to say, that can't wait until you sit down to work on your own fiction?

PH: Well, when he got the Nobel Prize, what they said was that he did a wonderful job of showing the hard features of the age, you know? It's a very hard century, the twentieth. Ask the fellows who dove into the water at the Chernobyl plant. There were a number who dove underneath to contain what was going on. It's been a hard century, and Hemingway was one of the people who really went in there. There's something extraordinary about artists. You have to take them seriously, and I think too much emphasis on biography and anecdotes tends to trivialize the artistic effort.

James Plath

Hemingway, with shark jaw, aboard the *Pilar*, Key West.

Courtesy of John F. Kennedy Library

GREGORY HEMINGWAY:
Gigi on Papa

Dr. Gregory Hemingway is the youngest of Ernest Hemingway's three sons, the younger of two boys by Hemingway's second wife, Pauline. Dr. Hemingway graduated from the University of Miami Medical School, earning his doctorate of medicine in 1964. He practiced family medicine in New York City, in Wyoming, and for ten years in Montana. Out west, he was the only family practitioner within a radius of seventy miles, and therefore, so as to be able to treat a variety of emergencies, was compelled to receive additional specialist training in cardiology and pediatrics. In retirement, he resides in Florida, and on the evening of this interview, July 31, 1998, he was at his summer home in Montana.

Frank Simons: Dr. Hemingway, as a boy, do you recall the circumstances of your father leaving Key West and moving to Cuba?

Gregory Hemingway: He was going to Cuba in the early thirties when he used to fish over there. I think it was about '34 when he first went over. And he went over mainly for the fishing. He also had a prolonged affair with a beautiful lady named Jane Mason.

FS: Were you and your brothers involved in a car accident while riding with Ms. Mason?

GH: I was allegedly in that car accident, but I remember nothing about it. I think it might have been my brothers Jack and Pat. I remember absolutely nothing about that.

FS: What do you remember of Ms. Mason?

GH: I remember she was a great beauty, and later saw pictures of her and was aware of how attractive she was.

FS: Was she a close friend of your father's?

GH: Definitely. They definitely had an affair, there's no question about that.

FS: Do you think your father was a womanizer?

GH: I don't think that's true. He was awfully shy, but someone like Jane, well, he taught her how to fish and everything, and I think he was able to overcome his shyness because she was just an absolute knock-out. I fully understand his being tempted, and not only that, but actually going for it [laughs]. I didn't know at the time that this was going on, and my mother must have felt awful about it. But Jack was often in Key West, and being older and in a better position of not actually being related to mother, he could observe my mother a lot better than I could, especially regarding Jane. When I was a kid, I never knew that there was anything going on, as Papa was quite discreet.

After the divorce I know it was said that my mother observed Papa in a photo of earlier years and sometimes would remark about how handsome he'd been as a young man. I think she was very much in love with him at one time.

FS: How old were you when he left your mother, Pauline, and, of course, moved from Key West to Cuba?

GH: Officially he left Key West in 1939 and I was about eight. I remember a little bit about it, but actually I was delighted, because my mother had been a very poor mother. She neglected me as a child, had me raised by a nurse, and she paid most of her attention to Patrick. So, for me, she was a terrible mother. A nice person, and everybody loved her, but she was just an awful mother, and I was delighted when he left there.

FS: Do you mean delighted for your father as well as yourself?

GH: Yes, there were no more arguments between them, and I liked my stepmother, Marty Gellhorn, a hell of a lot better than my own mother, which is a sad thing. Everybody needs a mother at an early age, and it certainly was the worst of all possible situations for me. But what the hell, you get over it.

FS: You recall in your book, *Papa,* of an incident of your playing loudly in the yard of your home in Key West on Whitehead, and consequently disturbing your father while he was working.

GH: Yes [laughs]. And this is a particularly forceful memory of a boy's childhood. Papa was upset with a disturbance while he was working. I was about four or five and was apparently banging on pots and pans or something [laughs], but he simply asked me to quiet down, "so a man can work!" But generally, he tolerated the racket, and for the most part, he was an excellent father. He just wasn't there. He was either in Africa making a safari when I was one and two, and then he was off to Cuba, fishing, and then from '36 to '40, he was mainly in Spain during the Spanish Civil War. So I saw very little of him. Nevertheless, I was crazy about him, even though I'd see him about a fourth of the time.

FS: Although your time with him was limited, you have a clear recollection of it?

GH: Oh, yes. It was a great time. He was a wonderful father and very attentive. Perhaps a bit too strict, too much discipline by today's standards. For example, he was a very good friend of Waldo Pierce, the painter. And Waldo had a couple of twin boys who were just about my age, maybe a little younger, because I was about four and they were about three. I remember my father buying us each an ice cream cone, and Waldo was working on a painting, and the twins took their ice cream cones and smashed them into the painting [laughs]. And Papa was just horrified. Waldo said to Papa, "It really wasn't very good anyway." [Laughs] I thought this kind of tolerance from Waldo would have been great from my own father. I would have loved that kind of tolerance, I think.

FS: *Islands in the Stream* is fiction, of course, and yet there are parallels to you and your brothers.

GH: Well, he does relate to us, but by God, he kills us off pretty early there, without much feeling.

FS: The setting for *Islands* is Bimini. Tell me of your experience as children while in Bimini or Cuba.

GH: In Cuba we had a lot of fun. It was a good experience, there were a lot of books around the house, and we read an awful lot, and when we weren't reading, it was a kids' paradise. We'd go out fishing, or go to the jai-alai or maybe go shooting at the Club de Cazadores, or down to the beach, just about anything. It was a great time. And you see, we'd always see him on our vacations, and he was always on vacation in the afternoon, because he wrote in the morning and played in the afternoon and evening.

FS: When you were a child visiting him in Cuba, he coached you for the World's Pigeon Shooting Championship.

GH: That was funny, and he was awfully good with that. I just had a great day that day, you know, like a hitter going five for five. I guess they call it being "in the zone" today. I couldn't miss anything, I just had it that day, and he recognized this and just left me alone and sort of acted like my manager. He got me drinks, Coca-Cola, and talked to me if I wanted to talk, and so on. A marvelous manager. I think he was very proud of me

FS: Your father wrote of the youngest son, David, in *Islands in the Stream* as having an instinct for cleverness and a coolness under pressure.

GH: I was good under pressure at shooting at a very early age. I was twelve when I was second there in the championship of the world in pigeon shooting. It was held in Cuba that year. So I was good then, and he was extremely proud of me. He loved a winner. He just liked anybody who was good at anything. You know, you'd be, maybe, the best axe-murderer of the world, but if you were the best [laughs], that's what counted, being the best at something.

FS: It has often been mentioned that he was particularly favorable to ordinary people, maybe even those who were down and out.

GH: I remember, there were several people who showed up at the Finca who were from Devil's Island. He put them up for several days, and they were extremely wizened, worn-out. Not completely beaten, but surely they had had a tough life for many years. I remember there were two of them and they were both quite small, and very soft-spoken. Papa was very polite to them, talked with them, ate with them, and they stayed there at the house for several days. Apparently they were, or had been, fugitives, if not from Devil's Island, from Cayenne.

FS: As you matured, becoming a young man, you did considerable hunting.

GH: I was just sort of doing what I thought he wanted me to do—a natural enough thing. And it was true, I think, that that's what he wanted for me. He perhaps would have preferred what I ultimately did in medicine, but that was all I was equipped to do at the time. I had a lot of trouble concentrating on my studies, so I went to Africa and became a professional hunter, and I think he became quite proud of that. He was aware of what I was doing because I used to write him, but we communicated less and less as the fifties got on. He'd just gotten in worse and worse shape and there really wasn't much fun at all towards the end from the age of fifty-eight on.

FS: What was your father's reaction to your entering medical school?

GH: Well, it was a little too late for him. He was pretty well going

Gregory "Gigi" Hemingway, with shark jaw, in the
yard of the Hemingway House, Key West.

downhill by then. But I remember I wrote to him that I'd just gotten
accepted into medical school, and he wrote back a one-page letter
and said, "I doubt if you'll have much success in your chosen pro-
fession, as I see you misspelled the word 'medicine'" [laughs].

At that stage—this was in the late fifties—he was in pretty bad
shape. He was drinking heavily, he wasn't writing much, he was

aware of his decreasing productivity, he had problems with his liver, and he was just generally bananas! And then, of course, he started to lose his mind in 1960, which was really tragic. He became paranoid and went out to the Mayo Clinic and had shock treatments.

FS: Your brother Jack mentions in his book [*Misadventures of a Flyfisherman: With and Without Papa*] that you and your brothers were allowed to sort of cut loose with some salty language and ribaldry after a day of hunting or fishing in Wyoming and Sun Valley.

GH: [Laughs] Gosh, I'm sure there were fun times like that. Papa was strict, but in some ways he could be very liberal with us. We'd all have a beer after shooting—even I at ten or eleven—and you know, you felt warm and cozy. But I don't think the swearing amounted to too much. At least I don't really remember much of it. But when we were all together there were some very good times.

FS: Can you recall your first meeting with Martha Gellhorn?

GH: Oh, yes. Marty was a lovely person. She just died recently—last year, I believe. She was a very good writer, very pretty, and a lot of fun.

FS: Did your father's relationship with Martha in any way impinge upon his writing career, as is sometimes suggested?

GH: I'm aware of that notion. That is really absurd. He was having his own problems. This was the first time in his life that I ever saw him irrational. And because of his problems, he was blaming everything on her. God knows why. I don't really have the faintest idea why he blamed her.

FS: During the Sun Valley years, while you and your brothers vacationed with him, do you recall his having to speak to you about the large tab you were running up?

GH: Yes, that was funny. And I was having a great time. I was about nine years old. And I remember he sat me down and had a talk with me, and said that I had to take it easy with the extravagant charges, the tickets I was signing, especially for the fancy lunches I was ordering, under glass and so forth, along with my regular trap shooting and tennis lessons. You see, the Sun Valley organization was comping Papa and us, and of course, Martha, during our stay there. I remember that Papa had said I had to be more careful, more conservative with this privilege, or they might ask us to leave. Of course, I don't think he meant that, but at the time, I recall thinking that if we had to leave, then who was going to feed the mallards that I'd been feeding every day as they swam in the pond there? It was a daily thing that I came to do routinely, and I was afraid of what would happen to the ducks if we were asked to leave. I guess I thought they'd come to depend on me, and they'd starve if I wasn't there to feed them [laughs].

FS: So your father was angry?

GH: No, not really. He was always quite decent to us. At one period, in '44, when he and Marty were having these terrible arguments and I just happened to be there during that summer, for the first time in my life he didn't make any sense. It was frightening. Of course, after the war he slowly went downhill. He could snap out of it and be extremely nice, but it was just a slow progression downhill. Most of his work after that, including *The Old Man and the Sea*, which I didn't think was all that great, was of lesser quality. All of his work, after that point, seemed to suffer. And he knew it! There was no better critic of his work than himself. Oh gosh, he couldn't produce anymore. A lot of it had to do with the drinking, but then, the drinking was kind of a symptom as well. It's hard to say which was which.

FS: Eventually, of course, the summer was over and you had to return to school in Key West.

GH: Yes, I hated for the vacations with Papa to end because it was such a good time, and it meant that I had to go back to school in the fall.

FS: Back in Key West, were you a celebrity's kid?

GH: No, not in Key West. Key West was an odd place. Even though everybody knew who he was and everything, I don't remember being treated any differently by friends that I played with, and I can remember my friends of that period in the third, fourth, fifth and sixth grades. I think, in that respect, it was a very normal childhood, a normal play group.

FS: Your mother, Pauline, never remarried. In your father's absence, whom did you look to for a role model?

GH: In a sense, Papa was always there. Somebody as strong a personality as my father may not be there physically, but his principles you interiorized, so you didn't need him to be there.

FS: Did your mother regularly contact your father should she have a problem or concern regarding you and your brother Patrick?

GH: Not that I was aware of, no. If you mean, was there a sense of threat or anything? No, not at all.

FS: I understand that your mother was a good friend of Lorine Thompson.

GH: Yes, they were extremely close. They could chatter women talk. Lorine was a real chatterbox. They would just talk for hours on end—come over, mainly in the evening, have a couple of daiquiris and sit by the pool there and talk. Back and forth to each other's homes, the Thompsons, the Chambers [Esther and Canby Chambers]. They had met the Chambers in Paris. And Mr. [J.B.] Sullivan, my godfather. They'd all come over and have frozen daiquiris by the pool. I remember that from around age thirteen until I went away to college.

FS: Apparently, you had a good father/son relationship.

GH: Yes, almost always long distance, sometimes phone calls, and we did communicate extensively up until about my becoming nineteen or so. I didn't see him much of the last decade of his life. As a matter of fact, I never saw him after 1950. But up until then, we were always communicating, either in person or by letter. He loved to write letters and receive them, and, of course, he sometimes would phone. So we were always in touch.

FS: When you were in your teens, was he advising you, much as a parent would, when a child might typically need counseling?

GH: Oh, yes. I can't recall specifics, but yes, of course, he was talking to me, telling me what was good and not so good for me.

FS: Your mother's marriage to your father followed Hadley's, Jack's mother, and after your mother, came Martha, and finally, Mary. Was it an awkward situation being introduced to your father's new women friends, particularly your stepmothers?

GH: I didn't think so at the time. I don't know just why I didn't, but to be honest with you, I didn't. Mary was just a new wife. I liked her very much at first. This was in 1945. She was full of life and wanted to do things, and I was quite fond of her at first.

FS: And later on?

GH: Later on, after he died and she inherited everything, I thought she was kind of a bore [laughs]. I think my brothers, Jack and Patrick, felt that way as well, although Pat took her out on safari in Africa. We sort of had to do honor to her because she was our father's widow, but none of us really liked her all that much, and I don't think it was just because of the money—although it would have been nicer if we'd gotten a bit more of the inheritance. Some people become sort of possessive, I guess. I'd hate to accuse her of it, but that may have been part of our feelings at the time.

FS: Your father wasn't at all awkward or shy when he introduced you to his new lady friends?

GH: He was actually shy about it. The initial introductions I can't remember, but I recall he was quite a shy person. Mary was living there at the house before they got married in, I think, '47 in Cuba [March 14, 1946]. But before the marriage, Mary lived at the Finca for quite some time. I liked her during all that time. The only thing was, Papa was beginning to go downhill. They would have some terrible arguments, just as he'd had with Martha. Again, I took her side. I had to, because I felt he was wrong.

FS: Were you ever in the position of having to choose between your mother, Pauline, and your father's later wives, Martha and Mary?

GH: No, no. They were there, and she was in Key West. And never the twain should meet [laughs]!

FS: How do you feel now, about your book, *Papa?*

GH: The book was as true as I could make it at the time. I wrote it in '75, which sounds like a long time after his death, but I was still very much under his emotional influence, and I think a lot more than I am now. I can understand some of the things he did much better now, and I don't feel quite so bad about them. I realize he was hurting and just about ready to kill himself, so he wasn't in any shape to deal with me or my problems. I can now look back a little more clearly, and I couldn't so much when I wrote it.

FS: You're a medical doctor. You were there a good share of the time. What is your understanding of why he chose to kill himself, if, indeed, it was a choice?

GH: I didn't understand at the time one of the really important factors of his life. One of the things that really drove him crazy over the years was the fact that his mother quite innocently raised him as a twin to his sister Madelaine for the first five years of his life.

This was quite innocent. Nobody knew about Freud in those days, but it was just a bone-crusher for him. He never got over it, I don't think. Somehow, this experience affected him throughout his life, all the time. There was a real tension about him as he got older that was really kind of frightening. And I think it had a lot to do with this silly thing that his mother had done to him. Of course, she didn't mean to hurt him.

FS: What diagnosis do you feel was appropriate for your father during his illness the last two to three years of his life?

GH: I know it's been suggested he was bipolar. "Bipolar" is a much-abused term. I'd say he was hypomanic, if you wanted to use any category, about ninety-five percent of his life, and then he got depressed right at the end. But I never saw him depressed—really depressed—in the years I spent with him. Never. I think the term "bipolar" applies quite well to some people. Josh Logan, for instance, was certainly bipolar—terribly manic, lost all judgment and everything. My father was never like that. He just had a hell of a lot of energy, so-called "hypomanic." There's no question that the last years of his life, the last eighteen months, he was clinically depressed. A depressed, paranoid schizophrenic. A lot of adjectives you could use, but I wouldn't use "bipolar," because most of his life he was hypomanic. This is not a bipolar personality. Please forgive me for being so definite about this, but I've given much thought to it, and the deterioration at the end was just classic paranoid schizophrenic. He felt everybody was out to get him. And of course, there was a tremendous physical deterioration, as well, that went along with it, and may have been part and parcel of it, but I just don't know.

I do know that at the Mayo Clinic his liver function tests were absolutely one hundred percent normal. It shows they're not all that sensitive a test, for one thing, because there were some times in his life when his liver function was terrible. Liver function, if you leave it alone, however—that is, not drink for a few months—in some people, some rare people, the liver comes right back to normal. I've seen his tests and they were perfectly normal. You think in terms of generalized deterioration of the man. I mean, he lost so much weight, down to 175 pounds or so, and he just wouldn't eat a thing. Then, of course, the shock treatments hadn't been completed, and it certainly was bad to stop them at that time. I still don't know how many he had. I think something like a series of thirteen, at first, and then, thirteen to fifteen again. I think he had completed that many series. And he was able to recover his memory. He wrote a very lucid letter to that doctor's son that was published in *Life* [Fritz Saviers, son of Dr. George Saviers of Sun Valley, who was hospitalized with heart disease. The letter was published in *Life*, August 25, 1961].

FS: While he was hospitalized at the Mayo Clinic, do you feel he was capable of manipulating the medical staff to his purposes?

GH: Well, yes, but not in the long run, because all he wanted to do was get the hell out of there and kill himself. But that's the trouble, everybody says, which has now become a cliché—that a celebrity doesn't get good treatment in a mental hospital because they are all in awe of them.

Frank Simons

Hemingway at Club de Cazadores in Cuba.

VALERIE HEMINGWAY:
Inside the *Cuadrilla*

Valerie Danby-Smith was a journalist working in Madrid when she met Ernest Hemingway in 1959. She served as his secretary in Spain, France, and Cuba in 1959 and 1960, and, after the author's death, worked for the Hemingway Estate in Cuba, Key West, Ketchum, and New York—gathering and organizing the author's papers, first for use by Carlos Baker, later for presentation to the Kennedy Library. She came by the Hemingway name by marrying—and later divorcing—Gregory, Ernest's youngest son. For two decades she worked in publishing and public relations in New York City, including two years as a fiction reviewer for *Publishers Weekly*. Her articles have appeared in *Saturday Review*, the *New York Times*, and *Ski Magazine*.

The interview was conducted on February 19, 1996.

James Plath: According to biographers, you met Ernest Hemingway in Spain when you were a nineteen-year-old journalist. Freelance or staff?

Valerie Hemingway: I was mostly freelance, although I worked for a couple of places. I was working for Belgian News Service at the particular time that I met him. I did a lot of English-language work for them, and they sent me to interview him.

JP: You got the interview?

VH: Yes, I did. You know, I didn't have any interest in Hemingway. It was just another assignment for me, so I had to go off and find out about him, and unfortunately the material I found on him was pretty out of date. But that's all right. I did it in English and then I handed it over to my office and I presume they translated it into French, because it would have gone over the air. It was a news service, you see. They would give me a list of questions they wanted me to ask. It wasn't just literary people, you know. In fact, he was the only literary person that I interviewed.

JP: He didn't grant many interviews. Did you manage to keep a copy?

VH: It's long been lost, because I was in Spain, left Spain, went to

Ireland, went to Cuba, went back to Europe, came back to America—so goodness knows whatever happened to it. At the time, it was not something of importance, because it never occurred to me that I would have any further association with him.

JP: Carlos Baker wrote that "Evidently, believing, as earlier with Adriana [Ivancich], that a miraculous renewal of youth could be achieved by association with a nineteen-year-old girl, he adopted Valerie Danby-Smith as his secretary, insisting on having her at his elbow during meals, at the bullfights, and in the car." First of all, is that the way you saw it? And secondly, could you comment on Baker's psychoanalysis?

VH: First of all, I didn't know anything about Adriana, and I was out essentially for myself—the way one is at nineteen [laughs]. I mean, I wasn't interested in other people's points of view.

JP: Did you sense any flirtation on Hemingway's part, or feeding off of youth?

VH: There were a lot of young people around. I met him in Madrid, and a couple of months later I went up to Pamplona at his invitation. I went up with a bunch of friends from Madrid, but I didn't realize until I got there that I was included in his party, you know. Basically, as I understood it, if you're living in Spain, one of the things you ought to do is go to Pamplona, and I thought, well, I probably ought to do that. And then I totally forgot about it. Other things came up in my life and I just didn't think of it again. Then I had a note from Juanito Quintana who said, "We've booked a room for you at Pamplona. Please let us know immediately if you can't come, because there's such a shortage of rooms there." I had actually moved addresses and so I didn't get this until much later, and there was a second letter there. It said, "Since we haven't heard from you, we now understand that you're coming up, and this is where your accommodations will be," and so on, and "meet us later." But even so, it still didn't occur to me that I was being invited as a guest of the party. I came from Ireland, where everyone helps everyone else. You don't think anything particular if someone does something for you that might be a little bit out of the way.

So I got up to Pamplona, I came on the train from Madrid with a bunch of friends and intended to hang out with them, but then I found that there were bullfight tickets there and a note where to meet the Hemingways and so on, so obviously I went off to meet them and thank them for the accommodations. And then it was sort of understood . . . I mean, I was sort of given my *schedule,* and I was paired up with a young reporter from the *Christian Science Monitor,* you know? We had our fight seats next to each other. And there were a number of young people there. I was not an exception.

How I became the secretary, at the end of the week everyone was planning the future and a lot of his guests were going down to Málaga for the famous sixtieth birthday party, and so he or Bill Davis said to me, "Are you coming down to the birthday party?" and I said, "Oh, no, I have to earn a living. I have to go back to Madrid and continue working." It was after that, Ernest sort of said to Bill, "Well, if Valerie has to work, why can't she work for us?" They went as a group, and he was staying with Bill and Annie, and he said, "Perhaps we could give Valerie some sort of work to do." And I was just dumfounded, you know? Bill said, "Well, I can't see why Valerie couldn't be useful. She can be the secretary to the *cuadrilla,*" as their group was called.

JP: That was the name that the Hemingway mob called themselves?

VH: Yes, named after the group in a bullfight: the matador and his *banderilleros* and his various men that worked around him. Hemingway and his little group, the inner group, were the *cuadrilla.* So, I went back and actually it was a fallow period, because in the summer everyone clears out of Madrid. It was July and I had planned to be away for August, so I began to think, what's the difference if I'm away for July and August? So I accepted. I went down and joined them in Málaga.

With Ernest, I think, as with a lot of men who don't want to accept getting older, I think they do sort of flirt with young people, there's no doubt about that.

JP: Oh, we finally got that one answered.

VH: [Laughs] Well, you know, I was not singular in that respect.

JP: All of the accounts and biographies tend to be narrative or factual in their orientation. I wonder if you could just describe, in some detail, a day at the bullfight with the Hemingway *cuadrilla,* or a typical day.

VH: Almost no two days were the same. In Spain, we were moving from place to place, unless there was a *feria* or fiesta, where there would be fights for three or four days.

JP: How about describing that first encounter with the Hemingway *cuadrilla,* then?

VH: First of all, I was a pretty independent person, so I didn't always follow the rules. I used to get into trouble occasionally for that. There were certain places we would meet, and in Pamplona—let me go back in my memory to that—it seemed to me that it was almost a continuous thing, where the night blended into day. You got three or four hours sleep. Two or three in the morning you're dancing in the street and having a merry time, and then you go to bed and you're up again and it would be ten or eleven when we met again in the square, and there would be the inevitable round of drinks, and the discussion. I mean, there always was a discussion, which was nice.

One of the things I spoke about last year in Key West was the learning process. That was one of the delights for Ernest and for young people to be around him. He loved to tell them about things, to teach them and to show them, so that we would meet somewhere between ten and eleven in the morning and sit mostly at the Choko Bar on the square. Then there would be a discussion about the day: the kind of day it was, the bulls and what kind they were, which *ganadería* they were from, and the bullfighters. Of course, Ernest was particularly interested in Antonio Ordoñez, and so if Antonio were fighting there'd be speculation as to what he might do with that particular bull, you know? There would be various serious discussions, but all the time there would be the interruptions, because young Americans, old Americans, and sometimes Spaniards, Europeans, and all sorts of people would come up and interrupt, *constantly.* Then we would have lunch before going off to the bullfight.

In some ways, it was fairly sedentary. Ernest would go—because bullfighting is essentially a man's sport, and women really don't hang around the bullring or the pen where they keep the bulls—especially if Antonio were fighting, he would want to go and actually look at the bulls. Often he would go off and talk to the other matadors. He would go and busy himself with that sort of thing. At that time, I don't think in Pamplona that I sat near him. He had

Hemingway instructs, Pamplona, 1959.

bought some tickets, but they weren't necessarily all together. I think in some cases I was a couple of rows behind, and I was to be with this young fellow from the *Christian Science Monitor* whose name utterly escapes me, and who was very *dour* [laughs] . . . He was certainly not an Irish, Celtic type at all, no one that I had been used to. He was quite put-out. I mean, I thought this was wonderful, in one way, to have these bullfight tickets and have this whole agenda which I hadn't even thought about. I thought I was going to have a completely different agenda, which would have also been completely interesting because the friends I had come up with were in the film business, and were making a film partly in Madrid and partly down in Málaga.

As part of that group I met Beverly Bentley, who later married Norman Mailer, and Beverly and I became great pals on this sort of *cuadrilla* circuit. In fact, in Valencia she and I shared a room. When she didn't have a room, I said, "Come and share mine." So I had an exciting bunch of people that I would have been with, had I not been [laughs] commandeered or whatever by this other group.

After the fight, we would again gather back at a bar, usually, and Ernest would go over the fight, pretty much movement by movement. And it amazes me, even now, that he was able to recall things. If you see a boxing match, can you recall every blow or every exchange? Not too long ago I was rereading *The Dangerous Summer,* and it was just incredible. We didn't have video then, not even in the papers do you get such detail, and he has these movement-by-movement accounts. He had an incredible memory.

JP: Would you call it photographic?

VH: I would think so, yes. He really had an amazing memory. But I don't know if he was accurate, because I can't remember those things pass by pass. If he made it up, it was exceptional, and nobody said, "That isn't the way it was." Today, you could do that, because you'd have a video of it, that if you didn't get it right someone could look at the video and say, "No, he didn't make that *veronica* up, he didn't do that." But it was just amazing. After each fight he would analyze it, what had been done wrong, what had been done right. And so it was just like an intensive course in bullfighting.

After that, we'd have a sort of break and plan to get together later and have more drinks and dinner, because in Spain they don't have dinner until about ten o'clock at night. And no matter where we were, dinner would go on for hours and hours. You had to have tremendous staying power. It was just unfortunate, in some ways, that I was so young and not attuned to a lot of the conversation. I had come directly from Ireland, and so I didn't know very much about American literary circles and literary gossip. I knew a lot about Irish literary circles, but not American. And also Hollywood, because in Pamplona that year David Selznick was supposed to be there. He was supposed to be in San Sebastian at the film festival, and the speculation was that he would be in Pamplona, and Ernest was still very angry with him about *A Farewell to Arms.* Ernest felt he got a very raw deal on it, that they paid him a flat $50,000, yet they made millions on it. He was very rankled about this. He wanted to capture Selznick and make him pay for his not being generous at the right time. So there were all sorts of asides like that.

JP: Did you attend the running of the bulls each morning?

VH: I didn't. I did get up maybe once or twice.

JP: Did Ernest?

VH: I think he did. First of all, he was not a person who slept very well, and he got up very early as a rule. I'm sure that he went, because that's where a certain amount of action was, and that was the first time you get to look at the bulls and get some idea of the breeds that were fighting that afternoon. He wanted to be a part of everything that was there, and of course he did, really.

When I got up early . . . I guess there was a certain part of the day when I avoided them. When I first joined, this idea of being there like twelve or fourteen hours of the day, I didn't realize that if you joined the *cuadrilla* you were on Spanish time. You were lucky if you got one half-afternoon off a week. You were expected to be there. Spanish servants are there from dawn until like two in the morning—they're still at your elbow, ready to fill up your glass. But I hadn't caught on, in Pamplona, because that was my first week. Also, I was there as a guest, or whatever, but not as a worker at that point.

JP: Sinatra had his Rat Pack, and some celebrities surround themselves with "yes" people. Others manage to attract genuine friends or pals, while still others are beset by groupies or wannabes. What was the Hemingway *cuadrilla* like?

VH: I think it was a mixture. I mean, there are always followers, the people who attach themselves like leeches, and they have their own agenda. It varied, because first of all there were Bill and Annie Davis, who were the Hemingways' host in Málaga. They didn't know them very well, but they were very rich and they had this beautiful house and lots of servants and serviceable cars, and when Bill wrote to Ernest and said he heard he was coming to Spain, could he be his host, maybe it's because he didn't know him very well that Ernest accepted. Mary always said she was very surprised, because normally they didn't stay at other people's houses. They either rented one or they stayed in hotels, for that independence. But actually it worked out very well, because Davis didn't intrude. He had a strange personality. It wasn't one of these effusive things. He was very much a laid-back, quiet, almost self-effacing type. Ernest called him "Negro" the whole time, because he had very thick lips and he felt he had this sort of Negroid . . . you know? So that was almost like using him as a servant, in a way. He drove the car. He was like the chauffeur, he was not so much like the host. He let the Hemingways use the house as if it were their own house. He didn't do the big thing of "I'm the host, I'm hosting the Hemingways." He really took a back seat, and his wife Annie was just the most delightful person, just a wonderful, warm person. There were two children who were about eight and ten or eleven at the time, so it was a family house. But the family was very much in the background.

Then, of course, there was the infamous Hotchner, who was invited as a friend. I think Ernest really enjoyed his company and did feel he was a friend. I mean, my only quarrel with Hotch was his writing a book when it was totally understood that friends did not write books. I mean, it was more than understood. You were told that if you want to be a part of this *cuadrilla,* then there were no books. So Hotch was there as a friend, and he was pretty much like the court jester. Ernest would bounce things off him. Ernest would say something and Hotch would counter it, and we'd all laugh. He had his position there.

Then Dr. George Saviers and his wife, Pat, came from Idaho, and again it was something that Ernest wanted to show them. It was part of his teaching. I don't think they'd ever been to Europe before—certainly not to Spain—and they hadn't seen bullfights and he loved to teach them. A lot of people who came to Pamplona and who were there most of the summer were personal friends who had been invited to the birthday party. But obviously, only people who had a certain amount of money and leisure time were able to do that. Another person who was a friend was Buck Lanham, and he was definitely a friend of Ernest's. And then when you sat down at the table, it seemed like there would be twenty there, because people would see you and they'd join. The table was large enough that people whom we didn't know at all could come and sit down; it would take a while for anyone to realize that they weren't a part of the official group.

JP: What about the journalists? Were these contingencies similar to press corps that would cover candidates during an election?

VH: No. He had some friends who were journalists, and I think he always wanted, as I think most personalities do, to be friendly with the press. There were some Spanish journalists there. There was José Luis Castillo Puche, I'm sure you know his book, *Hemingway in Spain,* and there were other people who came and went. Hemingway had been a journalist, and he definitely had a lot of journalist friends and encouraged journalism and felt that it was a very good way, if you wanted to write creatively, to get into that. He felt that if you wanted to write, that you should write in whatever form.

JP: I've read different accounts of his work day, in relation to other aspects such as fishing. What was your observation on his daily routine?

VH: Well, at the time I was with him he wrote every day. He wrote from early in the morning—I don't know what time he got up, but probably about six—until ten, pretty much every day. Sometimes a little later, if he was really going good, but otherwise he might even stop a little earlier. Then he had breakfast and he went swimming. The whole schedule was fairly regimented there. We went fishing on Wednesday afternoon and Saturday afternoon, unless there happened to be a squall or something that prevented it. The boat was ordered, the chauffeur was ordered . . . you know, when you have that kind of life where you don't do things spontaneously, because you've got a whole retinue of people who have to set it up for you.

JP: Did he need a nap in the afternoons?

VH: Usually in those countries you have a siesta, because we would have, usually, a bottle of wine with lunch, then after lunch there was usually a siesta. Then there would be another swim or some kind of activity. Sundays we went to cockfights. A couple of days a week Mary and I went into town. Once we went into the market, and then the other time we'd go shopping or for some other purpose. After the siesta, I would work with him in the afternoon. Then he would do letters and things like that, you know. Creative writing was done in the morning. And bedtime? In Cuba it was earlier—I would say around ten-thirty, eleven o'clock. In Spain, it was never before two.

JP: And would he be out there dancing in the streets with the others?

VH: He would be out there, yes, to a certain extent. He was definitely out there cheering other people on. In some ways he was a very shy person.

He always said he wasn't musical—and there was no evidence that he was musical—that he was forced to play the cello when he was young, and his mother emphasized music. Whether it was that he just decided he was going to take a lifelong dislike to it, or whether he actually didn't have musical ability, there were some things that he liked. He loved Fats Waller, and when we were in Spain around the pool, the Davises always had their loudspeakers by the pool and they always had Fats Waller songs. He loved things like "Your Feets Too Big"—that was one of his favorites. But as I recall, he did not really sing in tune. He loved to encourage other people to perform.

JP: You mentioned the sixtieth birthday party in Málaga. Legend has it that it was quite a blowout. Were you there?

VH: Oh, yes. It was an absolutely magnificent party. The house is a really beautiful house. The setting was lovely, and there were some very silly things there. For instance, they set up a rifle range, and in some cases there were caricatures of people Ernest didn't like and they were used as targets. Then there was a time when I think Antonio had a cigarette in his mouth—it got pretty wild—and they were trying to shoot the ash from the cigarette. Antonio's wife, Carmen, also had a birthday, although I must say she was rather secondary. The Maharajah of Cooch Behar was there, and the Maharajah of Jaipur and their maharanis, and David and Evangeline Bruce, all sorts of wonderful people were there, and some of them had flown in from all sorts of places. Some local Spanish aristocracy were there. There was music and laughter and fireworks— all that sort of thing. Again, that was pretty soon after I'd met him. I really only knew him for about two weeks at that point.

JP: What was your initial impression of Ernest, and did it change over the years?

VH: Initially I felt that he was very affable and kind, when I met him. I didn't even know if I would get the interview, and I was in a way surprised but not in a way surprised to—not because of him, but because I tended, if I wanted to do something, to find a way to do it. But I was pleasantly surprised at how, when I had that interview with him, he spent extra time chatting with me afterwards,

Photograph by Curvas, courtesy of John F. Kennedy Library

Hemingway's 60th Birthday Party, Malaga, sitting with Valerie.
The man dancing at left is the bullfighter, Antonio Ordoñez.

discussing me and my work and what I was doing, Ireland and his impressions of Ireland, Irish literature.

Usually, when I saw people, you just got the bare minimum and you went your way, so I thought that was good. At the time, Bill Davis was there and Mary was there, but there were other people around sort of walking in and out. Then, when I went up to Pamplona, it certainly was very jolly. It was a holiday atmosphere, not a working atmosphere. I had been to bullfights before, but I really knew nothing about them, so it was absolutely fascinating. He was, again, I thought, very affable. But he did, after a few drinks, as people do, go looking for David Selznick and [laughs] was going to pay him back for all the injury he'd received. I didn't think too much about that, because when you grow up in Dublin you meet a lot of characters and people do a lot of odd and strange things, and you don't even think twice about it, you know? So I sort of didn't judge him on that. We had a good week, and I must have liked it enough to say that I would go to Madrid and settle my affairs and meet them in Málaga.

I think just the change over the time was that Spain was a happy-go-lucky time. I know that there are other readings on this, and that there were certain tensions—in life there are always tensions. Yes, he got drunk, yes, they got drunk, we all got drunk at times, we all got on each other's nerves, and there were possible incidents. But that's life. That's just the way it is.

There was a real contrast between Spain and when I joined them in Cuba a couple of months later, because that was a totally different lifestyle. People didn't intrude. They had this place outside Havana which was on a hill, Finca Vigía, which means "lookout," and it was very peaceful. Ernest wrote every day . . . he wrote every day in Spain, but it was very hectic. This was very peaceful. By contrast, he didn't get drunk, there was no rowdiness, there weren't outbursts of temper. You know, the things that one associates with a lot of drinking: a lot of fun and then tension that results from it, and people milling in and out and misunderstandings of who's going to be where, when. In Cuba, everything was very, very regimented. Every night they had different people for dinner, but it was a routine. Monday night it was Cucu Kohly, who was a doctor (he had a lot of doctor friends), Tuesday it was the American ambassador, Wednesday it was Roberto Herrera, Thursday it was someone else, and Friday we went out to dinner. It was an absolute fest regimen. If anybody came, it was all pre-arranged. Obviously, you couldn't get in. The gate was locked, and there was no way you could penetrate the walls, so it was very ordered. Consequently, our lives were very low-key. It was really quite wonderful.

When I run into people who talk of Hemingway the drunk—including his sons—in Cuba, he didn't drink too much. We had a little wine at lunch—I doubt that the three of us had a bottle between us—and then the next drink was at five o'clock where you had one whiskey and soda or one rum and soda water with a piece of lime in it, and then we had dinner, you know, and we had wine with dinner and no drinks after dinner. So this idea of fall-down-drunk and one's brain being besotted certainly was not the case in Cuba.

JP: You did some of the typing on *A Moveable Feast?*

VH: I did pretty much all of the typing on that, and on *The Dangerous Summer.*

JP: Ernest was aware of Harold Loeb's own memoirs at the time, and that revisionist impulse in anyone who would recollect. Did Hemingway second-guess himself at any point during the writing of *A Moveable Feast,* or at any time during the writing indicate to you, off the record, that he might be having a bit of fun with the truth?

VH: No, because even though I say I typed it, he told me that he'd written it some time before. I've never quite pinned down when that was written. At one time he told me that he wrote it when he had a broken back after his second plane crash. I know he definitely told me that, because he said that when he was on his back he began thinking back to the early days, and that was when all this came to him. I don't remember him telling me, but I've heard from others that this was done earlier. And of course it could be that at one point he started it earlier, and then he seriously got down to it after the crash. When I was typing it, he wasn't writing it then. All he was doing was putting it in publishable form, because he had finally decided he would publish it.

He was really professional. By the time I typed it, he made very few mistakes. It might be a comma here and there, or an "and" or something, but there were no changes. He was amazingly disciplined in that way in his writing. I think the system that I could see that he was doing was that he would write every day. Supposing he got up with a filthy hangover (as people do) or you're just tired or you're sick. He would write no matter what. And I think the writing reflected that. I mean, there is some stuff there that's really almost bad. But that was just that he forced himself to do this, day after day. He never ever missed, when I knew him, and that was probably the worst part, in that he was older, he was disillusioned, he had suffered from depression and so on, but he always wrote. And when he was thinking of something for publication he was very careful, so that when he got stuff off to his editor in later years, there wasn't much that they changed. I mean, he would fight with Harry Brague, who was his editor at the time, over a word.

JP: Most scholars and biographers agree that Hemingway needed both romance and physical activity in order to get the writing done. In Cuba, did he maintain a physical regimen?

VH: He did swim every day, twice a day. We all had sort of allotted times when you went to the pool. Everyone went separately, and then swimming was usually exercise. It wasn't just lolling in the pool. I don't think we ever, at any time—Mary and I, or Ernest and I—were there together. We all went separately, and at least once a day. I remember Mary saying that for his birthday a couple of years before, a present she gave him was a truckload of ice. It was a very, very hot July, and so his gift went right into the pool. She was very big on birthdays and those kinds of celebrations.

I'm sure he did exercises in the morning, too, because every day on the wall he would put his weight, and he had his blood pressure taken frequently. He was *over-preoccupied* with health. That was something that was very important.

JP: Do you recall any boxing that he engaged in, either planned or spontaneous?

VH: You mean like altercations? I can remember going to find David Selznick, but we never found him [laughs] and so he didn't get boxed. In Cuba, it was a very regimented, quiet, and disciplined life. He was very wary of journalists, except for his personal friends, because he talked of the time a couple of years before, maybe '57, when Milt Machlin had come down, a writer of note at that time for *True,* or one of these popular pulp magazines. And he came down, he met Ernest at the Floridita. Nobody came to the house unless they were formally invited, because unless someone opened the gate they couldn't get in. But they met, and they apparently hit it off, and Machlin was invited to the Finca. He came, must have done an interview, because he had a little notebook, stayed to dinner, and they did have some drinks after dinner. In fact, Machlin was pretty stewed, so they poured him into his car or the chauffeur took him off. But the next day his little notebook was found in the sofa, and in the notebook he had just written these absolutely dreadful things—obviously as part of his article, instead of the answers—and Ernest was absolutely furious. Machlin would have been one of the people where, if he had run into Hemingway again—I think he actually had the effrontery to call the next day and ask, "Have you seen my notebook?"—he would have been a candidate for fisticuffs. That, I know.

JP: You worked for the Hemingway estate. Is that a euphemism for Mary?

VH: I don't think so, although it was Mary who paid me. The estate was working on the papers. I had an office at Scribner's, and all of his papers were put there. In fact, inadvertently, through that, Hotch got a lot of material for his book, because he used to come up and spend afternoons and we'd chat over things, and he'd say, "What are you doing now?" and I'd show him, because I trusted him, the same way Ernest had trusted him, you know? And I'd say, "Oh, look at this!" or "Can you imagine that?" because I had thought this was like being in the confessional. And, of course, Hotch used whatever he could of that material, which I thought was very rat-like. Anyway, I went through all the papers and prepared them for Carlos Baker, and later for the Hemingway library.

JP: Hemingway is known for being a pack-rat. Were there some unusual places where you discovered material?

VH: We went to Cuba, that was the first place, and we took out as much as we could or as much as we wanted to from there. Then we went out to Idaho, because those were the main places where things were. And then later Mary had me go through all the letters he had received, and I made a list and took the key thirty or forty people and I wrote to them and asked them if they would send Xeroxes of the letters they had received—and in many cases they had already gone to libraries, or had been sold. But in a lot of cases people did send us Xeroxes. So that was the "gathering."

James Plath

Kermit "Shine" Forbes and James "Iron Baby" Roberts, 1994.

KERMIT "SHINE" FORBES
& JAMES "IRON BABY" ROBERTS:
Boxing Ernest Hemingway

One of my greatest annual pleasures in directing the Hemingway Days Writers' Workshop & Conference in Key West was to spend time with two men who sparred with Ernest Hemingway on a regular basis from 1937 to 1939. I invited Kermit "Shine" Forbes and James "Iron Baby" Roberts to talk about their boxing days with Hemingway for the 1991 Hemingway Days Festival, and they quickly became favorites of workshop attendees—so much so that I asked them to return year after year. The conversations below are compiled from two summers of informal talks. The first conversation was taped on July 21, 1994—Ernest Hemingway's birthday. On the day after the boxers had spoken at the writers' workshop, I borrowed a pink "Conch Cruiser" women's bicycle from festival director Michael Whalton and pedaled down Whitehead Street, turned right on Petronia (where graffiti proclaimed I was entering "Bahama Village"), and bicycled past a police car that was pulled over to talk to several old black men in front of a bar. Roosters and dogs scurried in front of me across sidewalks, and in front of a store men sat on barrels playing checkers while others watched—worlds apart from the tourist traffic on Duval, less than a half-mile away. The exterior of Shine's house was decorated like the inside of a bar, with buoys, boxing gloves, framed newspaper clippings, plastic icons, and all sorts of odds and ends hanging on the walls. Iron Baby pedaled over on his own bike, and, seated on folding chairs in front of "Shine's Ponderosa," as a sign proclaimed, we talked about their boxing days with the man who would later win the Nobel Prize.

The second conversation was taped at Shine's Ponderosa on July 18, 1995, as the boxers worked with Hemingway look-alike Red Noyes, coaching him to fight as Hemingway did so that Shine and Red could stage a "bout" for workshop attendees. I was to act as referee, and Iron Baby was to work the microphone, explaining to the audience what it was like to fight Hemingway. Earlier in the week I had dropped by to set things up, and shared a beer with Shine in front of one of the neighborhood stores—his treat. As we talked, a police car approached and Shine cautioned me to work the paper bag up over my beer can so the label could not be seen. Moments later, the squad car gone, a fight broke out in the alley between two black teenagers who swung wildly at each other, not more than ten or twelve feet away from us. I took my cue from Shine, who leaned against the building, calmly watching, and finally told me, "They're just blowin' off some steam. That little fella has a pretty good left."

Born October 5, 1916, Kermit "Shine" Forbes ran away from home "with a cousin and a fella called the 'King of the Hoboes'" when he was thirteen, and ended up in Key West. James "Iron Baby" Roberts was born in Key West on September 26, 1920, and raised there. Times were hard and the men talked about selling Spanish limes for a nickel a bunch or diving for coins that tourists tossed from the piers. Boxing brought them together at what is now the Blue Heaven restaurant on the corner of Petronia and Thomas, and eventually landed them a job sparring with Ernest Hemingway five days a week helping to keep the writer in shape. Drafted years after Hemingway had left Key West for Cuba, Forbes ranked as a light-weight in the Army and won four championships while he was based in Macon, Georgia. Roberts, also drafted, won champion-ships and was a ranking light heavyweight during World War II.

James Plath: Key West boxing lore begins where the Blue Heaven restaurant is now located. What was it called during Hemingway's time?

James "Iron Baby" Roberts: The Blue Goose and Cup's Bar. The Blue Goose was a pool room downstairs and it had dancin' upstairs, and they used to carry whiskey, beer or whatever you wanted upstairs. There were also smaller rooms upstairs.

JP: According to Key West legend, it was a cathouse back then.

JR: No, no, no, no. No kinda way. Whoever told you it was a cathouse, they wrong.

Kermit Forbes: That was a tourist rumor. It was always a pool room, mostly, with rooms upstairs for private parties.

JR: When fight nights came on, nobody used the smaller rooms because the fighters used them as dressing rooms.

JP: The ring that was built on the side of the building, was that a portable, makeshift ring?

JR: No, it was a full-size, twenty-by-twenty canvas ring. It was a standard ring, and the ring was in the yard. They used to have anywhere from 300 to 500 people there. We had ringside seating and grandstands all the way around. Lots of people. It was white and black.

KF: People used to sit upstairs and watch, too, from the balconies.

JR: Every two weeks there'd be eight fights. Mostly Fridays, but sometimes on Saturdays.

KF: Fernandez used to do a lot of refereeing, and Hemingway.

JP: In *Hemingway's Key West*, Stuart McIver writes that grandstand seats were $1.25 and ringside seats were $3. Was there much betting, much money involved?

JR: No, there wasn't that much money, because it wasn't that much money in the community at that time. You take, for instance, Joe Louis, Sugar Ray Robinson, Henry Armstrong—all them big professional fighters—they had hell to make it back in them days. And when they got on the top, the money that they made back in them days was nothin' compared with today. For locals, it was that much cheaper. Twenty-five dollars was the most you'd get.

JP: I've heard that there was also a kind of fight where there were four boxers in the ring at once.

JR: That was for the teenagers. Bal Royal. You put four or five of them in the ring at once and you put on one glove on each one of them and blindfold 'em and let 'em go from there.

JP: What happened with the other hand?

JR: They keep it behind them. They can't use the other hand.

JP: And they just keep wailing the tar out of each other?

JR: Yeah, right, until there's only one standin'. Last one in, he's the winner. The winner would get donations from the crowd.

JP: Did you ever do that?

JR: No. I was way beyond that. Shine and I was the two best they had at that time.

JP: Tell me about when you first met Ernest Hemingway.

KF: We used to train up on Conch Key, and then come down to Key West every two weeks for the fights. Back then, my fightin' name was Battlin' Geech. A Geech is somebody who talk like he's from Carolina. They have white geeches and black geeches. And I was Battlin' Geech, and his fightin' name was Iron Baby.

JR: One night Black Pie, he fought a Cuban named Joe Mills. And Joe Mills could beat anything in Key West in his weight—and he didn't weigh but 114 pounds. He was a bantamweight, but he could take fighters twice as heavy as he was. When Black Pie fought Josey Mills, Josey Mills knocked Black Pie down.

KF: Five times.

JR: And every time he knocked him down, Black Pie'd get up. He knocked him down the first time, and nothin' happened. Then he come back and knocked him down the second time. Shine was the corner man, and the third time he hit him, Shine throwed the towel in. Hemingway, who was the referee, picked the towel up and throwed it back. Shine took and throwed it in the ring again. Hemingway did the same thing—throwed it back. Shine was on the ground, and the third time he throwed it back he got up on the apron of the ring. Then, when Hemingway throwed it back at him, Shine jumped through the ropes and was in the center of the ring with him. And when Hemingway threw the towel back at him a fourth time and hit him in the face accidentally, Shine swung at him.

KF: Black Pie was gettin' beat so bad, and I throwed the towel in. And when I throwed the towel in, Ernest Hemingway throwed the towel back out. He just wanted to let me know he was the boss of the ring. I throwed it back, and this time when he threw it, he hit me in the face and I jumped in there and I swung at him.

JR: Hemingway was facing him, but he missed Hemingway, because of Hemingway being so tall and Shine bein' so short and only weighin' 135 pounds.

JP: What were you swinging at, his belly button?

JR: [Laughs] No, he was swingin' at his head, but he had to reach up. He swung and missed and he landed up on his chest. Then he rested on Hemingway's shoulders and Hemingway grab him by the two ears and just held him while he kept tryin' to punch. Grabbed him by the two ears, and he couldn't do nothin' then.

KF: I could if I'da wanted to.

JR: [Hemingway] coulda ended it right there, because the policemen, they came in the ring and they wanted to arrest Shine.

90

They had about four or five policemen in the ring and Hemingway told them no. He say, "Any time a man have the guts to take a swing at me, you can leave him alone, it's alright. He alright." So they didn't bother him no more. Then we all got on Shine. Told Shine he was wrong, and Shine felt bad about it.

KF: When we got home that night, somebody say, "Do you know who it was that you took a poke at?" No, I say, I guess it's some guy what tried to fight one time, a bum tryin' to get a nickel or a dime to get a drink, or somethin' like that. Some old bum. And they say, "No, that's Ernest Hemingway, the big writer." I didn't know who he was.

JR: He looked like a common person. We didn't know he was a famous writer. He dressed on a casual basis. Khaki dungaree shorts, khaki shirts—this was the way he dressed. He just thought he was an ordinary person, and that's the way we took him. And the night that he and Shine threw the towel back and forth, all he was wearin' was a pair of old shorts and slippers. No shirt. So, I mean, we didn't know he was Ernest Hemingway, at the time.

KF: That night we all went to Hemingway's house to apologize.

JR: And this is how we came to get in touch with Hemingway. This is when Hemingway said, when he met us at the door, "I knew you all was comin'."

KF: We talked and he say, "Oh, forget it. I tell you what, though. Come over and you can train in the evening every day, as long as I be here."

JR: That's the way it end up.

JP: Where did he have the ring set up at the house on White-head?

JR: No ring. We just boxed outside by the swimming pool.

JP: Had you seen Hemingway referee before you had that encounter?

JR: Yeah. Every fight, he would be there.

JP: Really? And yet the *Citizen* mentions him only a few times. In the first brief mention, the January 6, 1937, issue reported that Ernest Hemingway refereed bouts. But the second mention is more detailed and more interesting. The March 19, 1937, *Citizen* reported that "Everything is ready for the big fight tonight at the Navy Field Arena. All the ringside seats have been sold and half of the bleacher seats have been taken so far," and that "Ernest Hemingway and

Harry Sylvester will be the seconds for [defending Key West champion Emory] Blackwell, and Battling Baker and Willie Jackson for [challenger Baby Ray] Atwell." The next day's paper read, "Blackwell KOed Atwell in third round last night. He was picked up by his seconds and by Blackwell's seconds and carried to his corner. He was out for about 10 minutes." Then readers were told that "In the semifinals . . . Harry Sylvester refereed for three rounds and Ernest Hemingway the other three." How was he as a referee? Did he seem to know what he was doing?

KF: Yeah, he did. He'd referee like any other referee. He'd say "Fight it out or break."

JR: He handled the fight good. He never let a fighter get hurt. He didn't believe in that. If he see a fellow in trouble, then he'd stop it. That's the kind of fellow he was.

JP: Except for that time with Black Pie?

JR: Well, he probably thought if he kept gettin' up he was okay.

JP: Tell me about the sparring. How'd that come about?

JR: He sent for us on Christmas Eve.

JP: The same year the incident happened with Shine?

JR: Yeah. The thing with Shine and Black Pie happened a little after Thanksgiving, and we heard from him next on Christmas Eve, 1936. We didn't have one penny in our pockets. Not one penny, and he made Christmas Day for us. He sent for us to come over and have some trainin'. He had some special guests. It was Gene Tunney, the retired heavyweight champion of the world, and he had one of the greatest lawyers in Key West over, lawyer Georgie Brooks . . .

KF: And baseball players. Professional baseball players were there.

JR: He had some more of the big people—we didn't know who they all was. He wanted Gene Tunney to look us over.

JP: Did you ever talk to Tunney?

JR: Oh, yeah, we had a conversation with him.

JP: How old were you both?

KF: He was seventeen or eighteen, and I was twenty-two or twenty-three, something like that. First it was Black Bob and Black Pie. After that, me and Iron Baby put on the gloves.

JR: Shine and I went three rounds as a boxing demonstration.

This was in the backyard, by the pool. The guests sit down and they was lookin' at me and Shine fightin' in a ring Hemingway had made.

KF: [Laughing] I hit Iron Baby and Iron Baby got mad, and he swung at me and he grunt, and everybody laugh like hell. If he had hit me with that blow, he might have knocked me over the god-damned fence.

JR: Yeah, I missed him. But we had a great Christmas. We got over two hundred dollars that night, and in them days that was plenty of money.

KF: In these days, too.

JR: In them days, the average salary of a black man was $14.50 a week. The average white man's salary was $35 to $40.

JP: Did Hemingway pay you, or did they pass the hat?

JR: Both. From then on, he would send for us practically every day, or every other day, and we would train with him. Every afternoon.

KF: Usually about three o'clock.

JP: Was his family there?

JR: His wife would be there, and the boys playing in the yard. But she didn't bother with . . . she was with her company. He had his, she had hers, and that was it.

JP: Were her companions more the society type?

JR: Lemme explain something to you. Back in them days, it was critical days because Key West was split in three sections. Take Duval Street east, and they call that Conchtown. From Truman Avenue to Division Street, that used to be Cuban Village. And Duval Street back this way out to Eaton Street, this used to be called Jungletown. A red-light district, mostly black and poor-white people.

KF: National Guard soldiers used to jump the fence at Fort Taylor and go there.

JP: Did soldiers and sailors go to the fights, too?

Both: Oh, yeah.

KF: Sometimes you'd have a soldier and a sailor fight, and sometimes a civilian and a sailor or a soldier or a marine. We used to go in the Navy Yard and fight Marines. In the Navy Yard you could, but you couldn't do it outside.

JP: At the Blue Heaven it was . . .

KF: Blacks against blacks. You had to fight blacks against blacks, at that time. Cuban Club? Blacks against blacks, or whites against whites. But if you fight on the Navy base, you could fight a white man.

JP: Did you like fighting on the Navy base, then?

KF: Well, we didn't get paid fighting on the Navy base. You fought as an amateur then. It was charity. They may give you a gift or something like that, but that's all.

JP: You said there were distinct sections in Key West, distinct economic levels, but what was life like between the races about the time you started sparring with Hemingway?

JR: We all acted as one. No one had no problem. It was a pretty good atmosphere. In Key West, black and white, we knew how to get along with one another. I think God blessed people in Key West because they followed the commandments of what God wants.

JP: What was the atmosphere like at the Hemingway house?

JR: It was a lively place, a lot of people. But lemme tell you this. Hemingway had a lot of good friends, black and white. I think me and Shine are the only two living [black men] who really knew him that well, but like I say, the man due some kind of credit. You have a park here named Jackson Square, named after a black man, and you had another square by the name of Pritchard Square, off Simonton and Eaton Streets, and I still feel like they should name that home he had "Hemingway Square."

JP: Have you read any of Hemingway's short stories?

Both: No.

JP: Some literary critics have been bothered by Hemingway's apparent ease in using such terms as "nigger" or "black bastard" to describe characters in his stories.

JR: Well he never used language like that.

KF: Wait, wait, wait. The reason that was used, that was in the story. He didn't mean no harm by sayin' it.

JR: I ain't never heard him use language like that, the whole time I was with him. Back then, use them kind of words and you woulda lost me, you know?

JP: So he treated you with respect?

KF: Yeah.

94

Home of Ernest Hemingway, Surrounded by Tropical Atmosphere, Key West, Florida   11

Vintage postcard, rear caption describes Ernest Hemingway as "author, war correspondent and big fish angler."

JR: We all got respect from him, and don't let nobody kid you on that.

JP: When you began boxing with Ernest Hemingway, did he get the equipment just to train with you guys?

KF: He already had it.

JR: The gloves that we used were training gloves. Sixteen ounces. He paid us to help him work out.

JP: How long would his workout be?

JR: It would be me, Black Pie, Joe Russell, and Shine. He liked to keep hisself physically fit. I'm tellin' you, he was pretty good.

KF: When we'd get over there [at the Hemingway house] we'd loosen up and hit the heavy bag, jump rope . . .

JP: And Hemingway would do this with you?

Both: Yeah, yeah.

JR: He'd be right there with us. This was an everyday thing, five days a week, to keep in shape. Physical fitness.

KF: Three minutes a round, and each one of us do from two to three rounds apiece. First Hemingway'd go with Joe Russell. Next it would be Black Pie, then Iron Baby, and then I would be the last one. Each one would be trainin' and one would be shadow-boxin' or jump ropes until you put on the gloves. And we'd just swing away with him and hit him and bounce off him [laughs].

JP: Joe Russell isn't the owner of Sloppy Joe's, right?

Both: No, that's Nassau Daddy. This Joe Russell, he's my brother-in-law. He named Black Bob.

JP: Everybody had a nickname. What about Ernest Hemingway?

KF: Papa.

JR: And like we was sayin', he stayed physically fit most of the time.

KF: Half the time, he don't mean to do it, but he was too rough for those boys. He'd pull his punches as best he could, but the boys couldn't take him. Josey Russell was twenty-two, twenty-five. He was fast, more slim than I was.

JR: He was the fastest.

KF: When he was in the ring with Hemingway, he'd hit and get away. Hit and get away.

JP: How did Hemingway respond?

KF: He never was a man gettin' around too much. He was a big man. He let us come to him.

JP: When would Hemingway tire?

JR: He didn't tire. Actually, he . . .

KF: He didn't move much, didn't do no footwork—just stood there [laughs] like an anchor. He stayed in the middle of the ring. I had to come to him. I'd circle him, and he'd turn with me. You'd weave and bob and he'd measure you up like this [extended left].

JR: He had those long arms. He'd get right up under the rib cage.

JP: Were there many knockdowns or knockouts?

KF: I think he knocked all of us down, but Iron Baby.

JR: I was the heavyweight. At that time I was close to 180.

JP: But still, you mean to tell me that a guy who reels in marlin doesn't have the arm strength to knock down a light heavyweight?

JR: He wasn't tryin'. He pulled his punches.

JP: So all the knockdowns were accidental?

KF: Listen, why he knock me and the others down is we're pushin'. We kept pushin' and he had to swing . . .

JP: Because you were in so close, and he had to swat you mosquitoes away?

KF: Yeah, yeah. He caught me, but he didn't stop me or nothin' like that. He just knocked me down. The gloves we had, you take a man pullin' his punches and you beat him all day long. The glove was so big that he mighta stagger or something like that. But he knocked me down—and he pulled his punches!

JR: [Laughter] He was a strong man.

KF: He told us to turn loose, but he pulled his punches.

JR: I wanna tell you this. The same gloves that Hemingway used to train with, they in the boxing hall of fame. Remember, we signed them?

KF: Yeah, yeah.

JP: How tall was Hemingway, and how much did he weigh at the time you sparred?

JR: He was well over six feet tall and weighed anywhere from 260 to 270. At that time I weighed 180 and [Shine] weighed 135. I was the heaviest of the bunch. I'm about 5'10" about that time, and Shine was 5'8" or so.

KF: But I was really fast.

JP: What was your strategy when you boxed Hemingway?

KF: Hit him and get out. We'd work in on him and get a lot of blows to the stomach. He didn't protect his middle.

JR: That's right. Get up real close because then he can't extend his arm, because his arm too long. Get in there, because if you slip up and you stay on, he'll pick you off just like a chicken pickin' corn. You had to stand off from him, because with his long arms he'd pick you to pieces.

JP: Did you ever see him knock anyone out?

KF: Not out—just down.

JP: Did either of you ever drop him?

JR: Jesus, no.

KF: You couldn't drop him.

JR: Not as big as that man was, no way, man, no way in the world.

KF: He was a good sport, though. He didn't get angry.

JR: No, no.

JP: Do you know of any times Hemingway put on the gloves other than to spar with you? Exhibitions or challenges?

JR: No, no. Just with us. Just for conditioning.

JP: What level was he at, really?

JR: He was a physically fit man, in his age-bracket—let's put it that way—because he was too slow and he couldn't move around like a light-heavyweight or a middleweight or a welterweight. He couldn't move around like that.

KF: You would have to handle him with a full-hand like that and knock that hand off . . .

JP: His blocking hand, his guard hand . . .

KF: And if you could get that in and work in and get a combination . . .

JR: Then you still ain't gonna do nothin' . . .

KF: 'Cause you couldn't shoot that long blow.

JP: Like Hemingway.

KF: Like Hemingway.

JR: But he'd miss a lotta times.

KF: A big man like him, you're fightin' men that are comin' in [close to the body], and so he had to come under with his blows.

JP: Talk about Hemingway's stance.

KF: He lean forward a bit, left foot forward, right foot back, and he held his left and right hands like this [left hand slightly higher]. He led with his left. He always kept his hands palm up, movin' in circles. Always.

JP: Forearms up to block the punches?

JR: Yeah, yeah.

KF: I would be in a deeper crouch, but Hemingway would bow. He'd be in a bow.

JP: He'd bend at the waist?

KF: Right. He was more of a slugger. He'd lead with his left, and then BAM.

JP: A roundhouse?

KF: Yeah, but his left would usually be a hook, not a jab. Left hook, then the right. And if we come in on him, he'd block the left, block the right, open us up, and then put one on the chin. But he always pulled his punches so he wouldn't hurt us.

JR: You see, he was a big, big man, and he coulda hurt us if he'd wanted.

KF: He rocked Black Pie one time, but then he said, "You sit down, Son, you sit down." See, if he hurt any of us, then he quit.

JP: Did it help you, as boxers, to train with him?

Both: Yeah, yeah.

KF: When we had a fight comin' up, then we had a place to train five-six days a week. Before we met Ernest Hemingway, we used to take clove bags and fill 'em up with sand and cloves, or we'd get a bag from the Marines and fill it up and we'd make a little gym right there where we used to fight at the Blue Heaven. We didn't have but one speed bag we had to take turns with, and so we did more shadow boxing than anything else. Until we got in with [Hemingway], and he had speed bags and a decent heavy bag.

JP: So it wasn't just you helping him train, it was the other way around, too.

Both: Yeah, yeah.

KF: In boxing, when you train, you train with a lightweight for speed, you train with a middleweight for speed, and you train with a heavyweight for stamina. I used to like to train with big guys, so that when I meet them small guys they look like nothin' to me. So yeah, it helped us, and we got paid too. He'd give us fifty dollars now and then. This was from 1937 to 1939.

JR: The experience and the rhythm and the knowledge that we gained was good, but I never dreamed that this man was the man that he is today. But he died a little too soon, because he would have joined Martin Luther King in his crusade. He was a courageous man and he was outstanding with the black community. You got some black people right now that's livin' who will tell you what kind of man this man was. Am I correct?

KF: Yeah, yeah.

JP: Did you guys get to talk about anything, or did you just box?

KF: We didn't have too many conversations. We'd train and he'd say, "You all be back tomorrow," and we'd say, "Yeah, we be back."

JR: One time he talked about goin' to Africa. He said, "But I'll be back." He said he was goin' to Africa because he wanted to learn the culture of the black people. This is what he told me. And he said, "I'm gonna do a little bit of writin', but I'll be back." So we said, all right. When he come back, we trained right on until he decided to go to Cuba.

JP: And did you see him again, after that?

KF: No, we never seen him no more.

JP: I've heard that Hemingway had parties where boxing was featured. How would that work?

KF: He'd have a party outside at night and we'd put on a boxing show. No ring most of the time, just right on the grass next to the pool. Usually they'd take up a collection for us.

JP: Did you ever have a drink with him afterwards?

JR: No, me an' [Forbes] never drink or smoke.

JP: His fictional characters talk tough. Was he a tough talker?

KF: No, not with us.

JP: Tell me more about the parties.

KF: He had a lot of big stars come down there.

JR: Big celebrities. We shook hands with them, but that's it. Some of the [other boxers] wanted to drink, and [Hemingway] would give them beer, but not liquor.

JP: How rough was Key West back then?

JR: Worse than now, but it was all right.

JP: Some Hemingway biographers have written that the bars Hemingway frequented were more rough and tumble than the bars today.

KF: Oh, they would have barroom fights, sure. Like right now, if me and you get into an argument, we lock up in a room and the best man win. No knives, nothing like that. Just fists. The policemen come along and say "What's goin' on?" and you say, ""We're fight-in'," and they say, ""Long as you don't cut one another or shoot one another, you can fight all day. May the best man win."

JR: One night, right around the corner from here, Shine argue with a guy who was takin' advantage of an old drunken man. Now, he has a buddy on the side, and he had this knife open. But he didn't know that Shine had a buddy too. And I took one shot at him, and when I took one shot at him, that was it. He was out like a light. And so the patrol of police came and he was stretched out on the bar with a knife in his hand. This was before the war. We explain it to the cops what happened, and they brought him to and took him away in the paddy wagon.

KF: All this boxing was before the war, when it was dog-eat-dog and thirty dollars was plenty of money.

JP: Was there any resentment of Hemingway for his leading a life of luxury while most people in Key West were struggling to make ends meet?

KF: No.

JR: No resentment. Lemme tell you somethin'. This man had enough money, he could have gone and built anywhere on the island. But he came to live in the black section of town, in Jungletown. And any time a man can leave a little island like this and go all the way to the continent of Africa and spread all his literature—everything that he write—to the world, he must be a great man.

KF: That's right.

JR: One of his best friends was a black man named Skinner, who was the bartender at Sloppy Joe's. This was some difficult times, because we were in the heart of segregation. But when a white man would get out of line in the bar at Sloppy Joe's, Skinner wouldn't have no worries, because Hemingway would take care of the whole thing. He cared about people. He was all right.

James Plath

Hemingway, mid-1930s.

L.T. CURRY:
Hemingway's Key West

Leonard Thompson Curry was born January 28, 1911, in "Conch-town" at 1108 Petronia Street. When I interviewed him on July 22, 1994, Curry was living in the Conch house his grandmother once resided in across the street—at the corner of Petronia and Ashe—a house he said was built in 1874 by the Johnson brothers, who also constructed the Oversea Hotel on Fleming Street between Margaret and Grinnell. Two stately Spanish limes shaded the entrance, and the brightly-tiled mosaic inlaid porch and front steps he said was typical of Conch house artistry. We sat on Curry's front porch while he told of his "minimal" contact with Ernest Hemingway and talked about Key West during the twenties and thirties. As the dockmaster during the time Hemingway lived in Key West, Curry logged the *Pilar* in and out. A distinguished looking man with a Faulknerian moustache, Curry smoked a pipe throughout the interview.

James Plath: You said that the brothers who built this house also built the Oversea Hotel, and that interests me because the Hemingway "mob" used to stay at that hotel.

L.T. Curry: That was an old landmark before it was torn down, and various big-shots used to stay there overnight. Even Babe Ruth set on that porch many a time, and we used to go down there when we knew he was comin'. He was very good with the kids. He'd answer questions, sit right around them on the floorboards of the porch. This was in the early twenties. He was down here a number of times, and the other greats, like Ty Cobb. They used to layover here, especially during prohibition, because they had a barroom close by and they could drink as much as they wanted when they were on tour.

JP: The Brooklyn Dodgers used to train in Florida, and I understand that they also took trips to Key West with the same kind of fervor as sailors on leave.

LTC: The Brooklyn Dodgers used to come here, and the Giants. You see, Babe Ruth was with the Giants in those days, so that's why he was there. You can get a list from the [*Key West*] *Citizen* of the teams that came here.

JP: Did they ever play exhibition games here in Key West?

LTC: Oh, yes.

JP: When Hemingway was in town?

LTC: No. This was long before Hemingway. But this was a great baseball and sporting town years ago. You had a very good field at the Army barracks and a quarter-mile cinder track. Then, at the old Athletic Club, at the foot of Duval Street, they had another baseball field and they also had a cinder track.

JP: What ran on that?

LTC: Track men. Olympians. But they used to play baseball too. Plenty of baseball players played here. During World War I, track stars went in the Army and they trained here, and the University of Havana runners used to come over for competition.

JP: One of the reasons I wanted to talk to you was to ask about a rumor about your beating Ernest Hemingway in a turkey shoot. If that's true, could you tell me about it?

LTC: Well, they had this turkey shoot to raise money—I can't remember who it was for—when I was working for WPA as dock-master. Major Ryan decided to have a turkey shoot to raise money for some charity. So plenty of people got together—National Guardsmen, old soldiers—and they decided they'd shoot. They knew I was fairly good with a rifle, so they asked, "Curry, are you gonna shoot?" And I said, "Yeah, if I can get a dollar." That was what it cost to enter. So I asked my daddy and he gave me one and I went down to Fort Taylor. They had a rifle range down there and we were firing 30-06 rifles. The rifles were furnished by the Army barracks, and they were zeroed in for 200 yards. They had been shot and zeroed in and cleaned without taking the setting off of them, because they had both types of sights on them. They had the leaf sight and the peep sight, and people were using them both.

JP: Anyone on the island could participate?

LTC: Oh yes, just so long as you paid the dollar to the Army. I guess a good forty people took part. I got two turkeys out of that.

JP: And Hemingway was one of the forty?

LTC: Whenever there was a sporting event in town, he was usually there. Hemingway and his companion, Charles Thompson. Charles and I were always good friends. Charles knew I could shoot.

Over-Sea Hotel, Johnson Brothers, Proprietors, Key West.

If I went down to the hardware store, don't get in the back there with Charles. "Come on," he'd say, "let's talk about this new bullet's come out." And Bubba, he'd have it. He was interested in these new bullets and rifles.

Charles Thompson shot that day, and Major Ryan came over to me and said, "Curry, Hemingway thinks he's gonna run us out of here." I said, "Well, Major, you the best." And he was the best sharp-shooter among the servicemen. And he said, "Look, either you or I has got to get him today, 'cause he's gettin' too braggadocious." He shot, then Hemingway shot, then I shot. And we were all three in the high 90s in the first round, all hitting bulls-eyes. Then we come back and Charles had been eliminated. And he tells Charles—again he's braggadociable—"I'll shoot him." And there was a little old Marine there, a good friend of mine. I say, "Are you ready to shoot today?" "Yeah," he says. So I said to tell them to put us together. I'll shoot first, and he'll shoot second. He and I made 97 out of a possible 100. Hemingway made 95. And Major Ryan shot 98. That's the way it ended. It ended with Major Ryan in First Place, and me and the other Marine tied for Second.

JP: And Hemingway got Third.

LTC: [Leans forward and lowers his voice] See, we were shooting with government rifles, but after the first round Hemingway went

105

and sent home for his rifle—which was all right, we didn't care. And then he started to shoot with it. In the second round, when we beat him, he grabbed the rifle. And you know those sandbags we were shootin' over? He was about to break his rifle over them when Charles Thompson grabbed him by the shoulders and put his foot behind his foot and threw him down and grabbed the rifle. He said, "What's the matter with you? Are you goin' crazy today?"

JP: Had you seen that side of him before?

LTC: No, no. He controlled himself. But, I'll tell you this. He was very good friends with Jerry Trevor, president of Florida National Bank. And the last trip that he made to Africa, he begged Jerry Trevor to get me to go as his gun guard. And then I come home and I tell my wife. She says, "Whatchu gonna do?" And I told her "I'm no fool. A man who loses his head at a rifle match, I'm not gonna go as his gun guard. He's liable to shoot me!"

JP: What was your first contact with Ernest Hemingway?

LTC: During the WPA was when I first contacted Hemingway, in the late thirties. He was fishin' down here quite a bit, and I was a dockmaster at down to what is known now as the Naval Station, and they allowed yachts or charter boats to tie up in there. Ernest Hemingway tied up there, so as the dockmaster I had to write him in when he came in and when he went out. He also had some very good friends down there, and they came in on a combination schooner and motor rig. The guy that had his boat, I had met him in Havana, Cuba, before he got here. He was a party-boat fisherman, he didn't speak much English, but he took care of Hemingway's boat. A little Cuban fella. I had met him when I was runnin' to Cuba on the S.S. *Cuba* back in the early thirties.

JP: Carlos Gutiérrez?

LTC: I didn't know his name. He knew me, but I didn't know his name.

JP: And your contact with Hemingway came . . .

LTC: It had to be the late thirties. Listen, lemme tell you somethin'. Personally, I didn't care to meet him. I did business with him, that was my job. But I didn't care for the man especially. I didn't like him. He was eccentric. And he'd go to Sloppy Joe's, and many's a time on Saturday nights he couldn't get a place to park on Front Street or Duval, so I'd tell him, "Oh, park it here in the Fire Station

L.T. Curry, Key West, 1994.

yard"—and the Fire Station was down at the old City Hall. I was also with the Fire Department back then. And he'd park in there. What little fussin' I had with him was all right, because we understood that was the way he was, and he did do plenty of good and he did help the boys with their boxing. He was a good boxer, and he trained some of the boxers here which were friends of mine. When they got beyond what he could teach them, he'd get somebody else to step in. And he would referee boxing matches and all that.

JP: How was he as a referee? Did you attend fights where he refereed?

LTC: Oh, yes. I guess he was as good as they come. He was really fast with his fists, especially for a big man. There were a couple around here who were faster than him, but he was really fast.

JP: Did you ever witness him get into any tough spots as a referee or watch him get into fights himself?

LTC: No. But I watched him spar just for fun at Rupert's Thirty

Acres, and also at the Key West Athletic Club, which was taken down during the last WPA. See, they couldn't keep it up. People down here couldn't afford a dollar and a half per month for membership, so the place deteriorated and they had to tear it down.

JP: Shine Forbes was telling me that in those days blacks were only allowed to fight blacks in public exhibitions. And yet Hemingway sparred with blacks. Did that raise any eyebrows?

LTC: No. Key West was more or less anything goes, but to put 'em on where it could be in the paper and all that, they wouldn't let that go. But if they wanted to spar, well he'd spar . . . and there were some blacks that they would allow in the Athletic Club. But it wasn't an institution where a black man could go and join. It was wrong, but what were you gonna do? It was the place and time.

JP: Did you ever talk much sports with Hemingway when he docked?

LTC: Nope. He didn't say much. He saw me sailin' one day and says, "I didn't know you sailed," and I said, "Well, I don't have anything to do. I was sailin' this boat, tryin' it out for this guy, and she runs kinda close, Mr. Hemingway."

JP: Close?

LTC: Close to the wind. And he says, "It looked like it." He knew, 'cause there used to be a guy who came down here with a two-master and he and Hemingway went out on that and they'd be gone for three or four days. And that guy could sail. Boy, he'd go right through that bight—he had no trouble, no matter where the wind was. He had power, but he didn't need it. He'd haul up his foresail—that's the sail that's amidship—and that's what he'd use to go out the bight with. Now, when he'd get out of the bight, he'd pull up his jibs and his mainsail and his topsail. And Hemingway, he knew his boats.

JP: How do you know?

LTC: For one thing, he didn't bump those docks too much. He came in, he'd bring her in and what you might call his number one man, Friday, would maybe sometimes throw a bumper out there so she wouldn't bump too hard, but that's all. And it wasn't too easy to do that, because of the way the wind would blow.

JP: What was Key West like during Hemingway's time there?

LTC: It was quiet. It was still plenty of houses down there, but

108

Pilar, docked in Havana, Cuba.

you've got to realize that they were mostly poor people. Times were tough, and there were always fund raisers for different organizations. And Hemingway, he loaned his house out for different affairs for organizations to raise money. I didn't attend them, because I wasn't makin' that kind of money. It was a nice place, and he kept the lawn well. I know you heard about his cats. Plenty of times we'd go out there to swim and the cats would all come out and sit and watch us. They had one there, he was like a dog. He'd jump out and swim when he wanted to.

JP: How often did the local residents see Hemingway about town?

LTC: Oh, he was all over town when he wasn't fishin' and he wasn't writin'. I think he must have done most of his writing in the wee hours of the morning, because we saw him around town an awful lot. Then he had his swimmin' pool there, and I was teachin' swimmin' for the Red Cross because I was trained at Rollins College for land, sea, and air rescue. That's why I got into that phase of the game, and I was around the waterfront quite a bit. I taught swim-min', and I taught some other things that I don't even like to talk about. I was drafted, same as everybody else. I don't like to brag, but I was overboard, I was shot at, I didn't get hit, and I didn't get cut. I had the long knife with me in case it was necessary, because we had German boats—submarines—landing right over on South Beach.

JP: So it wasn't a far-fetched thing, then, when Ernest Heming-way armed the *Pilar* and went off chasing U-Boats?

LTC: No, no! You didn't know! I can't prove it, because I never took no picture, but Hemingway had two-and-a-half-foot-long depth charges on board. He couldn't use the big ones. It was too much weight for that little boat.

JP: Did he arm it with anything else?

LTC: I wouldn't ask him. We were fightin' for our lives then, we thought. It was back then I trained draftees in Hemingway's pool. The secretary of the Red Cross called and asked if we could use his pool at nighttime. And Hemingway said, "Of course. Who's gonna be in charge?" "L.T. Curry," they told him. "That's all right," he said. And that was it. Two nights a week I'd teach there. He'd come out and look sometimes, but most nights he'd go inside the big house. When we started with these guys, they were plenty big, strong guys, but they couldn't swim good. I had to start from scratch with them. We started in the pool, and when they got good enough, then we'd go out in open water. I also had to teach them things I didn't really want to teach. I had to teach them how to knife fight in the water. And when they found out I could make knives, they kept after me to make them. I'd take big hacksaw blades and make knives out of them for everybody.

JP: So you were basically teaching swimming and guerrilla warfare in Hemingway's pool?

LTC: Yeah. I guess you could say that.

JP: But Hemingway wasn't involved, except to make his pool available twice a week?

LTC: No.

JP: What would it be like when Hemingway came in with the *Pilar*?

LTC: He'd leave around daylight and return anywhere from two to six o'clock. He always had fish. I have never seen him come in skunked. Some of them he'd give away, and some of them he'd tell the little Cuban guy to take care of them, and *Sí sí, señor,* Ernest Hemingway would go or somebody would pick him up and they'd go to Sloppy Joe's. One time he come by and said, "You know, somebody stole my bucket." And I said, "No, you left it on the dock. Here's your bucket." And I give him his bucket and he'd go down to wash the *Pilar.* You know he had two *Pilar*s. One caught fire over at the P&O Steamship Company dock, which was right next to where the airboats used to land for Pan-America. Well, he had permission, when there's no boats comin' in there, to tie his boat up. And there was an explosion one day—I don't know what happened—I think they gassed it up and then started the engine instead of waitin' for the fumes to blow out, and she blew. I ran over there with two CO2s, one under each arm, and they put it out. But it wasn't long after that when he showed up here with another *Pilar.*

JP: Did Hemingway have a routine when he'd go out and come in?

LTC: I guess he had a semi-routine, but he didn't have to be home except when he wanted to. So he left when he wanted and he came back when he wanted. Sometimes he had somebody with him, sometimes he went out alone. Then he'd come to Sloppy Joe's and stay there until Sloppy Joe's closed. Sloppy Joe—Joe Grunts, we used to call him—he knew Hemingway real well.

JP: How did Hemingway treat people in Key West?

LTC: Bubba, he was abrupt and he was rough, but if he liked you, nobody couldn't call you somethin' without him sayin' "Wait a minute!" Sometimes he liked you and you didn't even know he liked you until somethin' like that happened.

James Plath

Working a line: Carlos Gutiérrez.

JOE ALLEN:
A Game of Tenpins

Born a fifth-generation Conch in 1914, Joe Allen worked at *The Key West Citizen* as an office boy, then worked his way up to general manager before entering the Navy in 1940. After the war, he returned to Key West and published the *Coral Tribune* for five years, and at one time published five weeklies in Miami. After a stint as County Commissioner, he was elected and served in the Florida State Legislature from 1976 until 1986. His contact with Ernest Hemingway came when he was still a teenager, and the *Citizen* was only four pages long, with pages one and two devoted to news and editorials, page three to sports, and page four to society news.

Joe Allen: I was on *The Key West Citizen* staff working as an office boy. This was before television and extensive radio. Key West was a rendezvous for writers and news people who didn't get a vacation with pay. They got a vacation with a due bill. You know what I'm talking about? Times were hard, and newspapers generally didn't pay a whole lot. My salary was twelve dollars a week, and the man who owned the paper used to say that I had to be here before he got here and stay until after he left. Money was tight, so when the newspaper staff went on vacation, they gave them a due bill, which meant that they could stay at the hotel that advertised in the paper.

The Key West Citizen was located on Duval Street then, next to the corner where the art shop [Kennedy Gallery] is now on Greene Street. Next to the art shop was a two-story concrete building which was occupied by the *Citizen*. This was before Hemingway was actually famous. The people who came here—writers and newspaper people—came to fish, more or less. Most of them stayed at the Casa Marina, which at that time had a beautiful dining room and lobby and so forth, but the rooms were tiny, with three-quarter beds. Very small.

James Plath: European style?

JA: Yes, and the men often came here by themselves, without their wives. The wooden building across the street from the Casa Marina is where the hotel staff—waitresses and such—stayed. In those days, the summer vacation place was up in New England, and down here we were one of the winter spots, and any number of young women would come here to waitress. And the men came here on due bills. On a day when they couldn't go fishing, like on a rainy day, they'd come down to the *Citizen*. It was a hangout for writers and journalists. The *Citizen* was sometimes four, sometimes six pages. We put the paper to bed about three or four o'clock in the afternoon, if we were lucky, and Hemingway was one of them who would come over around that time to talk or shoot tenpins. Where the Bagatelle restaurant is now, there was an open-air tenpin alley, right next to the *Citizen*. It was called Al Mills' Tenpin Alley.

JP: Lawn bowling?

JA: Well, it's a small bowling ball they used in tenpins. The alley is exactly the same, but you use a small ball. We didn't have a bowling alley here in Key West at that time.

JP: Were the pins also smaller and narrower?

JA: Yeah. It was the same thing, only smaller. Hemingway liked to bowl—this was before he was famous—and he'd come over and try to get one of us from the *Citizen* to go with him and shoot tenpins next door.

JP: Did you bowl with him?

JA: Oh, of course. Many times. But I don't make any to-do about it.

JP: Hemingway was nearly forty at the time, and you were still a teenager. Were sports so important to him that he really didn't care what age his opponent or companion was?

JA: He was just an ordinary guy. Anybody that wanted to bowl, he'd go with them. All he wanted was somebody to go with him and shoot the tenpins.

JP: How often did he do that?

JA: I really can't say. Not frequently, but not infrequently. Whenever he'd get the idea to do it. Once or twice a month. But gradually he became famous, and then I had no contact with him.

JP: He stopped coming by the *Citizen* office?

JA: Yeah. He went into another area, you might say.

JP: So what was it like, bowling with Ernest Hemingway?

JA: [Laughs] Just like bowling with anybody else. Nothing special.

JP: When you think of Ernest Hemingway, what stands out in your mind? What do you remember most?

JA: He was just a plain Joe. An ordinary guy who talked about ordinary things. Nothing that stood out. He liked to joke, and he always seemed upbeat and full of energy—never a negative at all. No complaints. He lived in a world where everything was fine. That was my impression of him.

He loved Key West. He was wild about the city. He hung out at Sloppy Joe's, which is where Captain Tony's is now. But times were tough. I know, because my father was a merchant on Duval Street. Outside of Kresge's, we were the only other store of that type on Duval Street. We were a 5&10, but a minimum 5&10.

JP: More like a "3&8?"

JA: [Laughs] We sold radios and you name it, and we redeemed coupons. And when I got through at the *Citizen* I had to go home and help my father. [Laughs] It was a dreamy little town, you know?

JP: Key West was also a sporting town back then, wasn't it?

JA: Yeah, they had boxing, cockfights . . .

JP: Did Hemingway ever talk sports with you? Boxing, baseball?

JA: He liked baseball and he liked boxing. Around me he never talked about baseball, but he talked about the people who were boxing. But I can't remember what exactly he said.

JP: Did you ever go to the fights and watch Hemingway referee?

JA: Yeah, at least once that I remember. He was a big fella, the master of the ring. But that's all I remember. I never had social contact with him other than what I told you.

JP: What were race relations like at the time? Segregated? Integrated?

JA: Nobody thought about it. That was never a factor.

JP: Did blacks and whites interact?

JA: Oh, sure, yeah, definitely. They were mostly the Bahamian and West African Negroes, you know? And they were gentle and refined—very English—more like an English person in their mannerisms and talk and relationships with the white people. There was never any problem with race in those days. I don't remember a single incident where there was any race problem.

JP: What else do you remember about Ernest Hemingway?

JA: The owner of Sloppy Joe's, Joe Russell, was one of the few people in town who had a nice cabin cruiser. It was down there in the neighborhood where A&B Lobster House is located at the foot of Front Street. And Joe Russell moored his boat in that neighborhood. It was always stocked with provisions. He could leave the bar and cast off the lines and go out without having to do anything. He was Hemingway's man to take him fishing. Hemingway went fishing with Joe Russell quite a bit. Hemingway would stay in the bar and drink for a week, two weeks, whatever, and all of a sudden he'd say "Joe, let's go," and Joe would leave the bar in the hands of the black fella that worked for him and go out and cast off and go fishing. And Joe Russell told me—he was related to me distantly by marriage; my uncle Roy and he were brothers-in-law—that from the time that they would leave the dock 'til they came back and tied the boat up, Joe said there was never a word spoken. They had an agreement. That's when Hemingway did his thinking for his writing. This is what Joe told me—I didn't get it from Hemingway himself. But Joe had the boat that Hemingway fished on at that time. Joe would bait the hook and take the fish off the line and so forth, but from the time they left shore until the time they got back, they didn't talk.

JP: When you bowled with Hemingway, was there also no talking?

JA: No, no. He was talkative. But it was just normal talk.

JP: What about when Hemingway stopped by the *Citizen* office? Was writing or journalism ever discussed?

JA: No, just general conversation. I can't even remember what we talked about. But that's where the writers and newspapermen met in those days. There was no other place.

JP: Did Hemingway ever say what he liked about Key West?

JA: He just liked the flavor—it was an isolated town—and he liked the people. He liked Joe Russell and those other people he associated with down at the bars. At that time the town was poor, and there were maybe only 20,000 people—maybe not even that much.

JP: Some biographers have labeled Key West a rough town around that time. Would you agree with that?

JA: No, I wouldn't agree with that. The people here were more church-going. The town was full of churches. Downtown, we had the Fleming Street Church, the Star Church, the Baptist Church, the Episcopal Church, the Gospel Hall, the Congregational Church . . .

116

JP: Which is funny, because when most people think of Key West they think of bars.

JA: I don't remember too many bars in the city other than in the area where Sloppy Joe's was.

JP: What about traffic? Was it mostly pedestrian, auto, bicycle?

JA: A lot of bicycles at that time.

JP: Did Hemingway bicycle too?

JA: No, I don't remember him ever using a bicycle. As I said, I really didn't have that much contact with him. I don't want it said that I was a close friend of Ernest Hemingway, because I wasn't. I just bowled with him and talked with him and the others who dropped in at the *Citizen.*

James Plath

Photograph by Lloyd Arnold, courtesy of Forrest MacMullen

Snipe hunt, lower Wood River. Taylor "Beartracks" Williams, Forrest "Duke" MacMullen, and Hemingway, 1958.

FORREST MACMULLEN:
Papa in Idaho

I first saw Forrest MacMullen onstage at the Sun Valley Opera House, where he and other Idaho friends of Ernest and Mary had been assembled on a panel to talk to members of The Hemingway Society at their seventh international convention. MacMullen told me, "Papa used to say, 'I choose my own friends, they don't choose me.'" And MacMullen, despite an age difference of more than twenty-five years, was one of the people with whom Hemingway chose to spend his time in Idaho. Until he moved to Las Vegas in November 1960, MacMullen remained one of Hemingway's closest Idaho friends.

When it came time to end the panel session in Idaho, MacMullen told the audience that he would share with them the song that Hemingway said was his favorite—a tune he said was originally sung by Jay Fasset on Broadway:

> Saloon, saloon, saloon,
> It runs through my mind like a tune.
> I don't like cafes,
>   and I hate cabarets,
> But mention saloon and my heart runs away . . .

After one chorus sung by "Mac," the roomful of scholars joined in. This interview came two years later, on August 5, 1998.

James Plath: Why Ketchum? What was the attraction for Hemingway?

Forrest MacMullen: Well, I think the reason for Ketchum was that the movies were up there, the stars were up there, and Steve Hannigan was the publicity director for the Union Pacific and [Darryl F.] Zanuck had a hand in a lot of the stars coming up to Ketchum. And I think one of the reasons Hemingway came to the valley was for the hunting. This was the fall of 1939.

JP: I was just wondering why he stayed.

FM: I think he liked the people and he liked the area, and there was all kinds of hunting—like pheasants, ducks, once in a while rabbit shooting, and down around the Snake River Canyon there was good pigeon shooting down there . . .

JP: Although pigeons are dumb as buffalo. They just kind of circle around until you kill every last one of them.

FM: Yeah, pretty much the same. But they were a challenge as far as their erratic flying, you know.

JP: Who was responsible for getting the house and decorating the house?

FM: Bob Topping, and his brother, Dan Topping, who was the owner of the Yankees at one time. The Toppings were tin plate heirs, and Bob Topping built this house overlooking the Wood River, and it was built out of concrete. It was the same decor as the lodge was. And Mona Topping—Bob had to leave and go down to a warmer climate, and they moved down to Florida—Mona sold the house while Bob was in Florida. Chuck Atkinson was the one who finalized the deal on it. Topping had a trap field down alongside of the house, but the decor inside was more or less Mary's. Mary had done a wonderful job of decorating it. It was very comfortable and homey. You just felt at ease when you walked into the place. They had a TV set there, a big TV set, and we all used to go up and watch the Gillette Fight of the Week. Papa used to have his little notebook and a sawed-off pencil, and he'd take book on the fight just for fun—nothin' big, but we'd lay bets on it.

JP: How did you first become friends with Hemingway?

FM: I really became friends with Hemingway in '52 when we went down to Key West and then over to Havana. That's where I really first met him. Taylor Williams was more or less the one that took Elaine and Don and myself down with him to Cuba.

JP: So Taylor knew Ernest before you?

FM: Yes. Taylor used to wrap these deep-sea rods and he'd bring them down to Papa, and so when we left Key West to go to Havana we each took over two rods.

JP: In later years, did he ever talk about the Finca, the house he left behind in Cuba?

FM: Not too much, but he liked the Finca very very much. He was kind of removed from everything. Down on the flats—he was up on a hill—there was a big tin, galvanized dance hall, and once in a while they'd have dances down there and this Spanish music with all the trumpets and all that, and boy, you could hear it just like you was inside at the dance.

When we went down there—Elaine Perry, Don Anderson, and Taylor Williams (who's better known as "Beartracks") and myself—we left Key West and we flew into Havana and we checked into the Ambos Mundos Hotel. That's the one that Papa had stayed at several times and where he had done some of his work. Mary and Papa sent Juan, who was their driver, and he picked us up in the station wagon and took us out to the Finca. This was around ten in the morning, and when we got there Mary had a real nice lunch fixed for us. And we sat around the pool and had lunch and we talked, and Papa informed us that he had heard from Charlie Scribner, Jr., that he had accepted one of his short stories, *The Old Man and the Sea*. This was in May of 1952. We had a great time down there. Mary took us out to a couple of nightclubs, the Sans Souci and the Tropicana, and they were all outside. You were sittin' among the palm trees, and they had the big stage up there.

JP: Did Ernest go with you?

FM: No, he did not. Juan drove us down, and we went into the Sans Souci one night and the Tropicana the other. Prior to that, Mary'd come down and we'd meet her at the Floridita, where they made the fresh-fruit frozen daiquiris and they had a big spread there of stone or Morro crab on ice, and boy, was that delicious. We'd go from there to the nightclub, and they'd drop us back at the Ambos Mundos and then Juan would take Mary home.

JP: Why didn't Ernest go with you to the nightclubs?

FM: Well, he was never one to really go out nightclubbin', so we spent the time during the day with him. Mary took us to a jai-alai game too, and Papa had mentioned cockfighting, but they weren't doing any of that when we were there at that time.

JP: Any baseball?

FM: No baseball, and we didn't see any dogfights, either. We only spent two days in the afternoon with him and Mary, and the other days we'd go over to Cojimar and spend a couple afternoons over there. We'd go down to the Havana Yacht Club—the taxis were to the right of that—and we'd get in these little taxis. They'd seat about six to eight people, and we'd go across the Morro Bay right below the Morro Castle. We'd walk up a short walk and get on buses—typical

Cuban bus ride, with chicken crates on the top and pigs, and we were lost as far as language was concerned—and we'd go over to Cojimar. The drinks there were about fifty cents, whereas in Havana I think they were about two bucks. But we had a good time over there. That's where he had the *Pilar.*

JP: Moored at Cojimar?

FM: Yeah, and that's where they used to fish out of, and Mary's *Tin Kid* was moored over there too. That's the one she and Taylor went out big-game fishing in one time when Papa went out on the *Pilar,* on the big boat.

JP: Did she have someone sail it for her?

FM: No, she sailed it herself.

JP: Did you go out on the *Pilar?*

FM: No, I did not.

JP: You mentioned *The Old Man and the Sea,* and more than one person has claimed to be the inspiration for Santiago. Did Hemingway ever talk to you about who he had in mind?

FM: No, he didn't. But when Spencer Tracy made the movie they filmed a lot of it over at Cojimar, and Papa was very disappointed in Spencer Tracy's appearance. He liked his voice, but Tracy was bloated at the time. His hands weren't gnarled enough, he had fatty fingers and such, and Papa wanted an old man that was weatherbeaten.

JP: Was 1952 the only time you visited Hemingway in Cuba?

FM: That one time, in May of '52.

JP: Was he pretty happy to show you around?

FM: The house? Yeah. He took me up into the tower, and it almost looked like a big silo. Up on the top floor—I think it was the third floor—he had a mattress on the floor and there was a kind of tall-legged writing desk. That's all the furniture that was up in that room, and that's where he used to do a lot of his writing.

JP: Legend has it that he also stood on a kudu skin in his bedroom and wrote there as well. True?

FM: Yeah. And when they were in Ketchum, Lloyd Arnold had taken a writing desk and put more or less stilts on it to raise it up to where it would be the right height for Papa to stand and write on.

JP: What was his routine like in Idaho?

FM: Well, in the mornings, that was his time for his writing. He used to get up around five o'clock, sometimes earlier, depending upon how rested he was, and sometimes later. But it was six o'clock on the average, I'd say. He'd do his business in the mornings and then we'd usually get together if we were going shooting, which had been planned and that. We'd probably leave his house around ten or ten-thirty, and we'd go down country.

JP: What was a typical hunt like?

FM: Well, we made sure that our guns were in, that we had plenty shells, and there was a picnic basket, usually, with cold cuts, cheese slices, whole tomatoes, boiled eggs, salt and pepper shakers, a bottle of wine, knife and fork to spread the butter or mustard on the sandwiches, one or two loaves of bread, and we'd make sure that was all in the car and that our extra jackets were there. Then we'd head down country, and we're all yakkin' and such like that, having a good time talkin'. Don Anderson, and a lot of times Taylor, Tillie and Lloyd Arnold . . .

JP: Did you mostly jump shoot?

FM: Further down country we used to go pheasant shooting and we'd have to go up and ask permission from the farmer to hunt his fields. No matter how often we went there to hunt, we still had to ask every time. That was Papa's way of doing things. He wouldn't go into a field unless he had permission. Then we'd hunt the field. We'd kick the ditch banks or walk the wheat stubbles or the willow patches along the canals. If we'd see some ducks down along the canal—when I say "see," we'd get up on the banks and look down the canal, and you could see down so far—if the canal made a bend we'd mark that and go down shooting pheasant and then see if there were ducks on the canal. But we usually didn't mix the two together. There was pheasant hunting, and there were ducks.

JP: What was the etiquette? Did someone normally shoot first?

FM: Well, if you were in position, if a bird got up in front of you, you got it. Most of the time it was pretty evened out. Papa a lot of times would have Mary between him and somebody else—Mary, and, if she was along, Tillie Arnold—and Papa and maybe myself off on the other side, or Don Anderson or Lloyd Arnold. Then the rest of us would be strewn out on a line. To kick the fields out, we'd zig-zag down the fields and stop a little ways from the fence at the end of the field, make sure everybody was in line, and then we'd walk up very slowly. Usually at the end of the fence line that's where your birds would cower down and wait. Sometimes they'd spook before we got there, but in a lot of cases we had real good shooting at the end of the field.

JP: So there were no dogs to set the birds in flight or retrieve them?

FM: No. Most of the time we never did. One time we went hunting down in the Hagerman Valley with a fellow who had a Brittany spaniel. We had gotten through hunting and we looked around and there was no dog. And Papa said, "Well, we've got to go back and find him." When we found him, the Brittany was still on a "set," and it was a hen pheasant. We spooked it and we shot it, because Papa said it wasn't fair to the dog that had pointed and honored the set for that long and not get him something. We were out of line as far as the law was concerned—hen pheasants were unlawful—but we took the pheasant, and if we had gotten caught, that was it!

JP: Why did Hemingway call you the Duke?

FM: Well, when Papa and Mary had the Heiss house that they had rented—that was the first place they stayed when they came to Ketchum—they'd been there for a while and this one night I was down there, just Papa and Mary and I, and we'd had a real good dinner and some drinks. And Papa and I had been sparring in the kitchen, just open hands, and Mary kicked us out of the kitchen because she didn't want any of that ruckusing around her. And on the fireplace mantle there was a World War I bayonet, a good thirty inches long, like a stiletto. Papa said, "Mary, we're going to have to knight Duke. He can't run around here with a commoner's name." So he told me to kneel and he took the sword and put it on one shoulder and then the other and said, "I knight thee Duke." And from that time on everybody called me Duke.

JP: He used to love nicknames. During the time he spent in Sun Valley he often signed his name "Dr. Hemingstein."

FM: Yeah, yeah.

JP: What kind of things did you and Hemingway used to talk about?

FM: A lot of times when we were going down country it'd be just Mary and Papa and I. He always sat on the outside on the passenger side. Mary sometimes sat in the middle, or, if she didn't want to

Photograph: A.E. Hotchner. Print courtesy of Forrest MacMullen

"Mister Owl," Forrest MacMullen, and Papa. Ketchum, 1958.

be crowded, in the back seat. But he always had the windows down, no matter how cold it was, and we'd be going down country and he'd maybe remark about the ravens were out in the field in a flock, or there'd be a road kill on a rabbit and he'd remark about that. We just talked about what we saw as we drove along, and he used to make up songs as we were driving along—make the words up. He had a deep voice, a good voice. He'd see something—Mr. Magpie, or Mr. Crow, or Mr. Owl—and he'd sing about it. But mostly we'd talk about the surroundings and such.

JP: Did he ever mention anything about Cuba or any concerns he may have had?

FM: Yeah, yeah. He was worried about the Finca. He had a library of over 5,000 volumes when we were down there, and I understand now that they've made a museum out of it there's some 7,500 books. He got his guns out of there and got a lot of his mail out of there. I don't know if he had any money in Cuba. I think it was all Stateside. His concerns were that Castro's people wouldn't molest

125

the house.

JP: In the beginning, Hemingway was a vocal supporter of Castro. Could you shed any light on how his feelings may have changed? Did Papa talk about Castro?

FM: No. He was more concerned about the sugarcane workers. Batista had stripped them real good, putting everything into his pockets and bank accounts in South America or wherever he had them, and so Papa was concerned about the small guy.

JP: Did he think that the revolution would be good for the small guy?

FM: No, he did not. He was thinking that Castro would bring in a Communist set-up, and Papa wasn't for that. One time he told me that he was invited to go to Russia to hunt glacier bears over there, but he said, "I'm afraid to go, because I'd never get out of there." He was hoping that it would be better than what Batista had. He was more concerned about the people than he was about his own wealth—about the house, or his boat that he had over there, and such like that. I guess the Cuban people really worship Hemingway now, and they've got the *Pilar* in dry-dock now at the Finca.

JP: Did he ever talk to you about his work, or what critics had written about it?

FM: No, he never talked about his work to me—what his book was about, or such like that. He mentioned once or twice that one of the critics had put him down, and he didn't favor that too much. But he finally said, "I guess that's his opinion. That's his loss."

JP: In talking about his routine in Idaho, we kind of stopped at the hunting. What else filled his days and nights?

FM: Well, a lot of times we'd have trap shoots up at his house. We'd shoot upriver, where there was a big vacant expanse. We'd all put some money in the pot, and then the winner of the trap shoot would have to buy the wine for the dinner. Mary always had a real nice dinner. She was a gourmet cook, you know, and she always had a gorgeous set-down dinner. We'd be out there trapshooting until the light was gone, then we'd all go inside. The evening would go on until everybody had pretty much said, well, time to go. My theory was to leave while you're still having a good time.

JP: It sounds as if Mary and Ernest were social creatures, and that they may have spent more time with friends than they did alone, with each other.

FM: Oh, very much so. I'd say they spent at least three out of every seven days with friends, and that was the minimum.

JP: Everyone got along fine, no friction?

FM: Not much, no. I can remember the first time I got reprimanded by Papa. One day we were out hunting and shooting birds, and I'd yell "I got it, I got it." It didn't matter where I was at. I'd yell "I got it." And Papa said, "Duke, knock it off. Let 'em have the pleasure of thinking they got 'em." Mary usually always went with us, and Tillie, but there were also times we went by ourselves—like Papa, Lloyd, Taylor and myself.

Once or twice we ran into some snipe by accident. We were driving down the highway and Papa'd look down into the swamp area where there was ankle-deep water and a lot of watercress, and he says, "There's a big old mallard down there." So we turned around, parked, and walked down towards the mallard. The mallard got up and we shot at it, but we also spooked up all these snipe. We had a good snipe shoot. That's Wilson's jack-snipe.

JP: Talk about erratic fliers.

FM: Right, right. But we got about fourteen or sixteen that day, and we gave them all to Papa and he took them home and he had a feast.

JP: He'd need sixteen to have a feast. Those are small, small birds.

FM: That's what I'm saying. Sixteen was just about right for he and Mary.

JP: Did you ever go out as a group to any of the night spots in Ketchum or Sun Valley?

FM: When we'd go down country, on the way back we'd stop at the Snug Bar in Hailey and we'd have a few drinks there. The Snug Bar was kind of like a museum. There were a couple of old grizzly bear traps in there and all kinds of mining mementos. Al was the owner and bartender, and we used to go over and sit at the bar and have drinks and talk. There'd be cowboys and miners in there, and they all fit into the crowd. Papa would talk to all of them and ask them about their business. He was very interested in that aspect— the personality of a cowboy or a miner, or such like that.

There was only one time I can remember when we went to a

night spot. About '58 we went to The Ram at the Challenger Inn in Sun Valley on my birthday. I was about thirty-two, I guess, and the maitre d' had made up a menu for us. There was my mom and dad, Lloyd and Tillie, Win and Neets Gray, myself, and the Hemingways.

JP: What was Hemingway's personality like? Did it change at all in situations like that?

FM: It was just like being out with anybody else. He had a good time, he'd laugh and he'd joke, and as long as we were left to ourselves everything went fine. But if an outsider would walk over and make a comment or such like that, Papa would clam up until the person would leave. And when he was referring to somebody as being lowdown, he'd say, "They're lower than whale shit in the bottom of the ocean."

JP: And his interaction with celebrities?

FM: About the only celebrity that I was around was Gary Cooper, and hell, he fit right in with the group. One time we had this magpie shoot down at the Silver Creek clubhouse. Bud Purdy had a trap during the lambing season. He'd throw the carcass of the lambs in there after they skinned them and the magpies would drop through the top of this wire cage and then one guy would go in there with leather gloves and a gunny sack and grab these magpies and put them in the sack. Then we'd take them out on the dock of the clubhouse at Silver Creek and launch these magpies, and we'd shoot magpies. They have a very erratic flight too, you know. And Gary Cooper fit right in. He was shooting too. This one time that we were down there, Floss Atkinson and Mary cooked lamb fries and morel mushrooms and fried potatoes and onions and garlic toast—we had a real feed down there, and of course after the shooting we had our share of the drinks, too. Each person would have a favorite drink, like gin, or bourbon, scotch, or vodka, and they'd have two or three drinks. To be honest with you, I never saw anybody really get out of line at any of the drinking occasions that I was at.

JP: Everyone just got "social"?

FM: Let's say, "mellow."

JP: Did Hemingway say anything to you about the telegram he got inviting him to JFK's inauguration?

FM: Mary told me about that in a telephone call. I was living in Las Vegas by then. But Mary and I used to fight like cats and dogs because she was a Democrat and I was a Republican.

JP: And Ernest?

FM: He always kept out of it, where Mary and I were concerned. I didn't care for Joseph Kennedy's taking the wheat and making scotch out of it when it was supposed to go to Europe for bread. Things like that. One time, maybe I wasn't right, but I was arguing just to be arguing, and I said, "Oh, Mary, you're full of shit." Papa kind of gave me a side glance, and then later on he said, "You shouldn't have said that to Mary." And I said, "Well, I guess you're right," and I went over to Mary and apologized, and she acted like I hadn't said it. So we just dropped that.

JP: Speaking of cats and dogs, at the Idaho conference you mentioned that Hemingway used to bark at the mention of death?

FM: "Woof woof." That was more or less like a dog acknowledging that somebody had said something that was off-color to him.

JP: If in conversation somebody would mention death or the topic would come up . . .

FM: He'd say, "Woof woof." More or less acknowledging that he heard it. The first time that I was around him and death was mentioned and he said "Woof woof," I asked him about it. And he said, "It's an unpleasant thing. I have to hear those things," and I think he looked at death just like anybody else does. That was his way of acknowledging it.

Papa loved a good joke, and he especially loved this story I used to tell: They were having this funeral and the immediate family was sitting up front, as usual, and this drunk comes staggering down the aisle and wiggles in and sits right down with the immediate family. The young son says to the father, "Dad, should I get rid of him?" And the father says, "No, son, he's probably some poor soul that has some fond memories." So the funeral was over in the church and the immediate family got up to file out into the lead cars and the drunk follows the family out and gets in the car with them. They arrive at the grave site and the family gathers around the casket with all the other mourners out and around and the drunk is standing right there with the immediate family. The minister gives his sermon and at the conclusion he reaches down and he grabs a clod and crumbles it on the casket. He says, "From dust thou were, to dust thou shall return. The Lord giveth, and the Lord taketh away." With that, the staggering drunk turns around to the congregation and says, "Say, folks, if that isn't a square deal, I'll kiss your ass."

Another thing that we used to talk about, Papa and I, was that he envied the mountain men back in frontier days. He always said that he sure wished that he could have lived then when the mountain men would come in to the spring meeting where they'd bring their furs in and they'd have their drinking and their shooting sessions. He thought they were something else. Up there all winter, snowed in, some of them had squaws and some of them didn't. I don't know what his fascination was, whether it was coping with the loneliness, or what, but he envied the mountain men.

He also would talk about his childhood once in a while and I'd talk about mine. And he'd say, "I can understand what you're talking about." It was a case of maybe a dad hugging you or a mother hugging you, which, evidently, he never got. There was a lot of aspects of growing up I think he missed once he found out the others were getting it. His mother giving him love, you know?

JP: He never felt loved by his mother?

FM: No, and then of course his dad was busy with his doctoring. After his dad's death, his mother gave Ernest the revolver that his dad had used. And I still maintain that Papa's death was an accident too, because when Papa left and went down to Cuba for the last time, I sent the guns—five guns—to Abercrombie & Fitch. Papa told me we're gonna have the swivel taken off of the front barrel and the swivel off the rear stock, then he says the trigger pull's awful stiff on it, tell them to have that honed down so it's not such a stiff trigger pull. I did that, and the gun was never the same when he got it back from them. You could drop it and it'd go off.

JP: You said you thought his death was an accident too. Did Ernest think his father's death was an accident, rather than suicide?

FM: Somewhat, he did. Yeah. And I still think it was an accident with him. I can't see it, somebody saying he put his big toe in the trigger and he went that way. I still maintain that he dumped the butt on the floor and it went off.

JP: Carlos Baker reports that Buck Lanham, seeing Ernest in 1959, was "sorrowfully struck by Ernest's unhealthy nostalgia for his young manhood and the astonishing obscenity of his language."

Did he strike you that way?

FM: No, no. I would have to say that Buck Lanham, at that particular time, they might have been like two grizzly bears in the same cage. If they had any kind of disagreement, they were both at fault. At that particular time they kind of grated on each other. Things used to grate on Papa, but he never carried a grudge.

JP: What were some of the things that grated on Hemingway?

FM: Well, if we'd go out hunting and somebody did something wrong. Like the time we were driving along the ditch bank and A.E. Hotchner was along with us. Hotch was on the outside and Papa was sitting in the front. Papa said, "There's some mallards up ahead in the canal. Don't look at them, because it'll spook 'em." And, of course, a lot of times it would spook birds if you looked right at them. Hotch didn't pay any attention, and that grated on Papa. He said something to Hotch about it.

JP: Did Ernest talk with you about his failing health?

FM: Nope. He never dwelled on it with me, as far as his feeling bad.

JP: Did Hemingway ever share with you what he considered an ideal workspace?

FM: Well, he enjoyed looking out the window, looking at the surroundings. You wouldn't be going out into space daydreaming if you didn't have something to look at. He used to watch this kingfisher that used to sit up on a dead limb of the big cottonwood tree down by the river, and there's a pool underneath the limb that this kingfisher used to sit on. That kingfisher used to sit on that limb for unlimited lengths of time, and suddenly he'd drop off with his wings folded and go down. Maybe he'd come back with something, most of the time he didn't. But the kingfisher was fishing for fish down in this pool below Papa's writing desk, and Papa was always betting on the kingfisher.

JP: *Time* magazine named Hemingway one of the hundred most influential people of the century. Does that surprise you, or was there something about Hemingway that even his day-to-day friends saw that made him different or special?

FM: He was special to me because he treated me as a man and he liked my company as I liked his. He was a gentleman's gentleman. He always had conversation with me, but I felt that I was on his level.

JP: Despite the age difference?

FM: Yeah, well, one time Mary and he and I were in the car and he said, "Duke, I think Miss Mary and I ought to adopt you." So I think he looked at me more as a younger brother. I'm proud to have known him. In the middle sixties, I became very good friends with Erskine Caldwell and his wife, Virginia. One time, when he was in Vegas visiting, I asked him, "Erskine, did you ever get a chance to meet Hemingway?" And Erskine had a real, fine dry sense of humor. He said, "No, I'm sorry, Ernest Hemingway never had the pleasure." I always thought that was cute. I'm not taking anything away from Erskine, but Hemingway was so much bigger as a novelist than Erskine.

James Plath

Photograph by Lloyd Arnold, courtesy of Forrest MacMullen

"Duke," Papa, and Pete Hill.
Christmas 1959, at Papa and Mary's House.

BUD PURDY:
Across the Creek and Into the Night

One of Ernest Hemingway's Idaho friends, Bud Purdy met Hemingway when the author asked him for permission to hunt on his ranch near Silver Creek. And that "yes" turned into a twenty-year friendship.

Bud Purdy: You gotta go back to 1939. I'm a rancher here in Picabo, Idaho. We have a pretty good-sized creek—stream, really—running through the property and there's a lot of ducks here. He started coming down here in '39 when he was up in Sun Valley. I didn't know him really well back then, but I got to know him. And he fished here at that time. I never fished with him, but he fished here with his two smaller boys, Patrick and Gregory—Gigi, we called him. Then he came back in the fall of 1940, I think—I've got books he signed for me, "nice duck hunting" and things like that with the dates in them, that I could always refer to—but we became pretty good friends then. Chuck Atkinson, a fellow that worked for me, or for my family—we had a general store here—he was a great hunter and so we all became friends of Papa, as we called him. (I called him Ernie part of the time.) That was our relationship. We hunted ducks here different times, and hunted pheasants about thirty miles from here down in another area. I knew him until he died, and towards the end we were really good friends. But the fact that I would duck hunt with him, that established our friendship.

We were social friends of his too. He'd have a party or, he liked the Friday night fights and he'd invite everyone over to watch. This was when he was renting the Heiss house around 1958. And then he stayed at the [MacDonald] cabins one fall [now the Ketchum Korral]. In fact, he was there at Christmas time.

When he had the Heiss house, he picked up an owl one time that was winged, and he tried to nurse it back to health. So when he'd be down here and we'd be through hunting, he'd say, "Well, we gotta shoot a blackbird for the owl." So we'd sit around here. Blackbirds would fly over about dark, and we'd shoot a bunch of them for the owl. [Laughs] He used to do crazy things like that.

He got us shootin' magpies. We was trappin' magpies because at that time there was a bounty on them, and we had a trap that we'd drop down on them and there'd be maybe fifty or a hundred that would get in there. He'd say, "What are you gonna do with those?" Well, we just, you know, let the kids go in there and wring their necks. He said, "Well, let's catch 'em and shoot 'em like clay pigeons. So a couple of falls, maybe a little longer than that, we'd set these traps and then we'd have a magpie shoot. And he organized it. You wouldn't do that now, of course. I think they're protected.

James Plath: Even if they weren't, the animal rights people would be after you.

BP: Oh my God, you couldn't even think of it. They're migratory birds, I guess. But back then they were a predator. They were hard on ground-nesting birds, for one thing, and they had a bounty on them. But anyway, he organized it, and we'd have a shooter and then we'd have a couple backer-uppers. We always got the kids to go in there and sack the magpies up and then they'd throw 'em. A lot of 'em got away. They're hard to hit.

He organized a big jackrabbit hunt too, one year when he was here late, well into January. He furnished the 12-gauge shotgun shells, and there were about twenty hunters, a lot of them movie people. Gary Cooper was along, and there were other prominent movie people. Hemingway went down the country about thirty or forty miles from here where the jackrabbits were really thick. So he had about twenty of us all lined up. I think we shot about five hundred that day. He was quite a hunter, and quite an organizer.

Cooper was around here a lot. He and Hemingway were friends, and we were friends of Cooper's. He hunted with us quite often. He was here late in the fall for that, and his wife liked to ski so he was here in the winter. We'd also throw hand-traps. We had one place we'd throw hand-traps out. We'd bet a dollar a trap. Hemingway'd always beat us, of course. He was a good shot. A really good shot.

JP: You said Hemingway was an organizer. Was he also a social organizer?

BP: I don't think that much. He was a hunting organizer. When we'd shoot ducks, there might be three or four people he'd bring along. We had places we jump shot—that means you walked up on them and shot 'em when they took flight. He was the one who

Magpie Shoot at Silver Creek. Gary Cooper, Bud Purdy, Papa, Bobbie and John Peterson, Ruth Purdy, "Duke" MacMullen.

organized everyone: you be here, you be there, and then we'll march up there along these ditches and get there the same time. That sort of thing.

JP: Mary wrote in her book that they also canoed the Silver Creek area to jump shoot.

BP: I never hunted with him in a canoe. He did that early on, in '39 and when he came back in '40, '41. They'd get in the canoe and float the creek and they'd shoot the ducks as they'd go around the bend. When he got down to the lower end of the ranch he noticed one afternoon that these ducks were flying over a certain ridge, a low ridge, and he told us all about it. He was leaving, but he thought we'd have good hunting there. So there was about ten of us up there shooting ducks on what turned out to be the day Pearl Harbor was bombed, December 7, 1941. That was one of his discoveries, that the ducks were flying up over this ridge. He showed us where they were. Just like when my wife and I wanted to go to Africa to see my brother in Nairobi, he told us how to get there. He told us the way

135

he went down was he went to Venice and got on the boat and went to Mombasa. He thought it was a great trip. That was the same time he got in the airplane wreck there. He planned our whole trip. He gave us a note to give to the bartender at The Ritz bar in Paris, and we thought we'd get a free drink, but we didn't. It was almost "So what?" Maybe we didn't get the right bartender. But he mapped out our whole trip for us, how we got to Mombasa, Kenya.

JP: Via the Ritz Hotel?

BP: Yeah, and then we had to go in a bar in Venice, same way. He knew the bars everywhere, I'll tell you. We had a note for that bar too, but we just didn't seem to get anywhere with those notes.

JP: [Laughs] Maybe he had outstanding bar tabs.

BP: Yeah, he mighta had a bar tab. He wasn't a really rich guy when he first come up here, I'll tell you. He was living off the cuff in '39. But as soon as he got some of the movie money, I think then he started doing pretty good. Then his books were starting to make money.

JP: Did he ever talk about the movie treatments of his books?

BP: No, he didn't. He was just that kind of guy.

JP: What about Pearl Harbor or his desire to reenter the war arena as a correspondent?

BP: You know, he never talked much about the war, or Castro, or politics. He was pretty quiet on those subjects. He had the house in Cuba at the time, but he never talked much about it. He never talked about what he was writing, either. [Laughs] He wanted me to come up to Ketchum and have lunch with him one day and we went into a place called The Alpine. He said, "Oh, wait a minute, I gotta go over and get a bottle of wine." So he walked across the street to the liquor store and we sat there. He said, "Boy, I sure had a great morning. I wrote a thousand words, and it's worth a dollar a word." He was pretty sharp in those days. But about three days a week he'd have to come down here and shoot ducks.

JP: Was that for recreation, or relaxation?

BP: I think both. He just needed to kind of do it. He'd bring a few guys with him once in a while. He brought Hotchner down with him once. Hotchner didn't really like to hunt ducks, but he was working with Hemingway on a few projects, and so he had to come down.

JP: What was the attraction of bird hunting for Hemingway?

Why not big game in Idaho?

BP: Well, he shot big game mostly in Wyoming, I think. I was never around him when he shot big game. And of course he shot a lot of big game in Africa. But shooting ducks and pheasant, it's a real sport. He just enjoyed it. He liked to get out and physically do things. He liked to get out and walk and tramp around. He was a physical guy. As he got older he couldn't do quite as much as he wanted to, but that's what he liked to do.

JP: Rumor has it that you used to get up in an airplane and spot ducks for him.

BP: [Laughs] Yeah. I had a little old Piper, and he'd say, "I'm comin' down," and I'd say, "Hell, I'll get up and see where those birds are."

JP: His request or your suggestion?

BP: I'd do it. He wasn't afraid to get up in an airplane. He went with me one time, but usually I'd just go spot 'em—there was always two or three other guys along—and then we'd go jump 'em up. It made it easier hunting. But he wasn't afraid of airplanes. You probably know the story of his African plane crashes. The wreck in Africa, it was reported that he was killed. He got in this plane and he told me that the guy took off in a rough field and didn't get off good. Then they sent another plane over after him, and it crashed. He had two crashes in one day.

JP: Now when you took him up in your little Piper, was that before the African crashes or after?

BP: This was before. After those African crashes, I think it hurt him. He had a head injury, and he changed appearance awful fast from when we first knew him. His beard became quite white. Of course, he told my wife that he had a skin problem—that's why he let his beard grow—and that's probably true.

JP: But after the African plane crashes he was never really the same?

BP: I thought when he came back he wasn't quite as sharp. You know, he was always good to people, though. I never saw him brush anyone off at any time. You'd be out eating with him and some guy'd come up—they didn't bother him too much up there [in Ketchum], really—and he was always nice to everyone. But he liked the out-door guys more than anyone—the hunters, the fishermen—and he liked the Basque people, too. There's a lot of them around here—sheepherders, bartenders, and bar owners.

JP: Would he speak Spanish to them?

BP: Well, yeah. He spoke pretty good Spanish. He was in Cuba all that time, you know. I think he liked this country because it reminded him of country in Spain, where he also spent time.

JP: What was it like being around Ernest?

BP: He was a lot more relaxed when he was with a couple of us than he was with a large group. He was a very outgoing guy, though. He'd go up there to The Ram in Sun Valley and have a big dinner and a lot of people around him. He liked to do that. When you were with him one-on-one he was fairly quiet, except talking about where the ducks would be or maybe talking about some hunting. That kind of talk. But he never really talked about what he was writing and never really talked politics. He kept away from that.

And we never. . . People say he was an alcoholic. Well, that was wrong. He wasn't that. You know, we'd go hunting and there'd be three, four, five of us, and we'd hunt till it got kind of dark. We'd get through hunting and we had a little cabin there and we might sit down and have a few drinks and cook some ducks, something like that—but he wasn't doing any drinking in the morning or afternoon until he got through with what he was doing. He did enough drinking after hours, but anyone thinks he's an alcoholic, I think that's wrong.

JP: What are the memories that stand out most in your mind?

BP: Oh, I took him over east of here and there was a little old creek. We were just looking around and we had the guns and I said, "We'll just walk down that creek. I think there's some ducks down there." He was ahead of me, and three ducks got up. He had three shells in his pump shotgun, and he shot all three of them. [Laughs] That was pretty damn good! Gettin' all three of them, bang-bang-bang, he was really happy to do that.

Another thing I remember, when he first come out here in '39, he had a convertible Buick. I wasn't with him, but he and a guy from Carey, a hunter, they got in that Buick and started down the country to go pheasant hunting. But I guess they ended up turning it over on the gravel road on the way down [laughs].

He'd usually get up here fairly early in the fall and stay up here

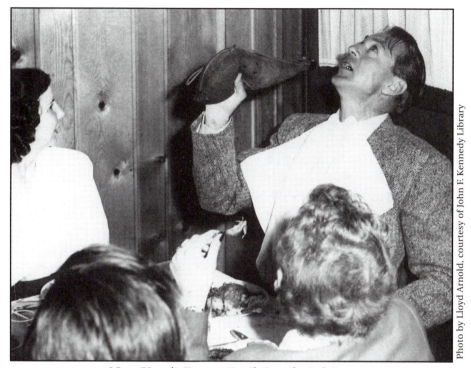

New Year's Eve at Trail Creek Cabins.
Gary Cooper demonstrates the bota.

Photo by Lloyd Arnold, courtesy of John F. Kennedy Library

until after New Year's and then take off. Sometimes he'd leave a little earlier.

He was always glad to see you. He was out of here for quite a few years. We didn't see him until after the war, and we walked in The Ram at Sun Valley and he was there and Mary and, God, he was just so glad to see us. It makes you feel good when someone puts himself out a bit, someone like him.

I remember one time, the summer before he died—before he shot himself, I should say—I don't know why he did it, but he invited all of his hunting buddies (there must have been eight or nine of us) up to his house there in Ketchum. There's a porch on that house and he invited us for lunch. We had a nice lunch—Mary was there— and he said, "Let's shoot some traps." Well, today you couldn't shoot a trap off of that porch because you'd hit someone. But he had fifteen acres there, so we threw hand-traps off of that porch and shot

139

'em for a while. And that's probably the last time he had a group around him, I suppose. We took him out to dinner just before the second time that he went to Mayo, and you could see that he wasn't really himself. He was uncertain of himself, really concerned about people sitting behind us. He got worrying about the Internal Revenue people for some reason or other. That isn't a fondest memory, but it stands out. And then he went back to Mayo and came back and that was it. But up until the time that he started having mental problems, every morning he was working.

JP: Did those mental problems start after the plane crashes, or after his Mayo Clinic shock treatments?

BP: After the Mayo Clinic, the first time. They didn't tell me what all they did. I wish old George Saviers were here. He was his doctor, and he took him back there twice. He died about three years ago—really great friend of mine, great guy. He really knew Hemingway.

One thing that's kind of interesting—I don't think it makes any difference now—you know that gun he shot himself with? The sheriff was a friend of Chuck Atkinson that worked for us, and Chuck's the one who got the house for Hemingway. Bob Topping was out there, and he was a big drinker, he was, and he built this house to look like Sun Valley Lodge over on the river, and Chuck found out it was for sale—I think for $50,000, fifteen acres, which, I guess at that time, was a lot of money—but he got Papa to buy it, which was really a good thing. It made him a nice place the last two years of his life. Anyway, the sheriff got the gun—he went up there after Hemingway shot himself—so Chuck talked to the sheriff, Les Outes, a good friend of ours, and he told Les, "You know, we ought to get rid of that gun." And so they took a torch to it and cut it into little pieces, and then they buried it.

JP: You're kidding. Really?

BP: Well, you never heard of the gun, have you? You never seen it, have you? You look into it and see if that gun's anywhere. [Forrest MacMullen confirmed in a follow-up phone call that the gun was disposed of in the manner Purdy describes].

I got a gun that Mary gave me. She gave me her Mannlicher that she used in Africa to shoot when they were over there. She willed that to me. I think that was a Model 12. It always seemed like she shot a pump gun.

JP: And the gun he killed himself with is buried somewhere in Idaho?

BP: It's buried somewhere. I think it was a good thing. That thing doesn't have to hang on the wall somewhere.

JP: Did Hemingway ever tell you about the gun he got from his mother—the one his father used to commit suicide?

BP: No. I wonder where that gun is?

JP: I don't know.

BP: Well, you might find out, but I'll bet you no one knows where that gun of his is that he shot himself with.

JP: Fascinating. What other memories do you have?

BP: It's hard to remember, but another one was, we're sittin' in my house—I guess we had gone hunting or something—and I said something about *The Old Man and the Sea,* and he said, "Did I give you a copy of that?" I said no, and he said, "I want to make sure you get a copy of that," and he signed it for me. That was kind of special for me. He's a great guy . . . but he was twenty years older than I was. I'm eighty now.

JP: You said he never spoke about his writing. Not even *The Garden of Eden,* which he was working on in Idaho?

BP: No. He was pretty quiet about what he was doing. I don't think anyone knew what he was writing. I don't even know if Mary knew what he was doing.

JP: Did you ever share your reaction to his work?

BP: *Green Hills of Africa* I did, because I was over there, and he told us all about Africa. He told us to go down and see Patrick, who was living in Arusha at the time. That's one of his better books, as far as I was concerned, because of the hunting in it.

JP: And you told him that?

BP: Oh, yeah. I can't remember what he said, but he seemed to be very pleased.

JP: Did you ever hunt with him when he was with his sons?

BP: No, they weren't out here that much, except when he first came out here. He took them fishing, but I was never with him. And later on, they never were here at all. Patrick moved to Arusha, and we went to see him down there. Gigi was trained as a doctor at the time.

JP: What was a social event at the Hemingways' like?

BP: Several things. When he liked the Friday night fights, there'd be eight or ten people there and he'd have drinks for us and serve some nice food. One thing that happened—and it isn't funny, either—he wore those granny glasses and he had a pair setting on the mantle, and I was throwing my arms around, talking, and I knocked them down and broke them. You know, you'd think that'd make a guy mad or something, but no, he said "Don't worry about it at all, I got another pair." It didn't phase him a minute. He was a gracious host.

But he didn't like the government people too much, I can tell you that. He was always making fun of bureaucrats. He didn't like them; he was always suspicious of them, for some reason or another.

JP: Republicans or Democrats, it didn't matter?

BP: Like I say, we didn't get too much into politics, but he was more of a Democrat than he was a Republican. He kind of liked John Kennedy, and I think that was part of it. But for someone who won the Nobel Prize, he never really talked much about those kind of things.

One thing he did, when he come up to Sun Valley he attracted a lot of people here. John Huston and a fellow named Jim Agee who worked for *Time* Magazine, and Leonard Bernstein was up here one day and wanted to see him. You just didn't know who was going to come around.

JP: Sun Valley still maintains that kind of glamour, doesn't it?

BP: Yeah, and Hemingway had a lot to do with it. He didn't fall over those kind of people. It was the other way around. He and Cooper were good friends. Cooper was kind of a hunter too. He'd come out here in the fall and he'd go around shooting hawks off the electric wire crossarms. Boy, I tell you, you wouldn't do that now . . . you wouldn't even think of it.

They gave a couple parties together. They always had a big New Year's Eve party if they were up at the cabin around that time of year. We were up to one of them. They'd have old Van Johnson, he was kind of a star then, and Ingrid Bergman and her husband, Merle Oberon, Claudette Colbert, and I can't remember who else. John Huston came up a couple times. He was quite a guy.

JP: Were the New Year's Eve parties wild, tame, or somewhere in between?

BP: They were just nice social gatherings. Have a few drinks and eat—a lot of fun. That's mainly what it was.

JP: In the fall of 1946, Cooper and Hemingway were both in Idaho to hunt, but there was also a special showing of the Burt Lancaster movie, "The Killers," at the Sun Valley Opera House around that time. Did you or the Hemingways attend?

BP: I don't remember. You know, I told him one time, I said, "When I was in college, one of the short stories we had to read was 'The Killers,'" and he got a kick out of that. But I don't know if he was there or not. I forget a lot of things. That was a long time ago. You know, we were hunting pals, but we were good friends too. I felt like I could call him up and talk about whatever—though we didn't have much of that going on—but I could call him up and invite him to dinner. We did do that quite a lot.

JP: Did he confide in you in later years?

BP: Well, he wasn't the kind of guy that was confiding in people. He never talked about his writing much.

JP: Did he talk about problems, gripes?

BP: Nope. Not too much. And he didn't talk about Castro, either. I think he wanted to stay in good with Castro and didn't want to get crossways with him, because he had a house there.

JP: In the beginning he was quite a supporter.

BP: He was. The poor downtrodden guy, that's who he cared about. All these movie people and all those didn't impress him. He wasn't caught up with them at all. He was equal to them and more so. Towards the last, he was a pretty famous guy, but around his friends he was just a normal guy.

The last time I hunted with him was the fall before he shot himself. He'd come down with Dr. Saviers and we'd kinda gone along this canal looking for ducks. I was always the spotter, the guy who always looked down the canal to spot 'em, and one time he said, "I'd sure hate to be a duck and have Bud Purdy lookin' for me" [laughs]. We saw a bunch of mallards on this one bend, and it was getting dark. I think there was eight ducks there, and I hate to say it but we shot all eight.

JP: You "hate to say it" because that put you over the limit?

BP: No, because I don't hunt as much as I used to. I like to see 'em rather than shoot 'em. But that was really something. He couldn't believe that the three of us shot all eight ducks, and just before dark, too.

I had an old Chesapeake [retriever], and sometimes Hemingway had his car and he'd be driving that old car. It wasn't a pick-up, so the dog had to ride up front. God, he'd be wet, and naturally had to almost sit in Papa's lap. But he didn't bother him a damn bit. That was okay with him, because he retrieved the ducks, I guess. He was a very easygoing guy, the way I knew him.

JP: You never saw him lose his temper or mistreat people?

BP: I won't say he didn't, but I never saw him. [Pauses] It was bothering him toward the last when he couldn't be the macho guy he wanted to be. [Laughs] You know, he thought he was a prize-fighter early on.

JP: Did you ever box him?

BP: No, but my brother-in-law and him, we'd had a few drinks, we were up in the cabin, and my brother-in-law's about his size. God, they got to shoving each other around a little bit, and I'll be damned if I know why. Probably just too many drinks. Well, it was just for a minute. No punches. They were just kind of up against each other. But he liked to think he was a kind of prize-fighter.

They weren't fall-down-drunk parties, just nice drinking parties. He was a great wine drinker and he introduced us to the bota. I think he also introduced wine lifters to Sun Valley. You ever seen a wine lifter? They put a bottle of wine on the table and you put your glass under it and fill it up. I don't see them anymore, but it's a great way to drink a lot of wine.

But he kept his business life and his personal life separate. He was just that kind of guy. He never confided in me. I'm not saying he never confided in anybody else. Just with me. But there's a lot of people who knew him better that I did. George Saviers was one of them. Clara Spiegel is gone. She knew him better than I did. She died this year. They're all dying off. There were five of us on the committee to erect a Hemingway Memorial at Sun Valley, and there's two of us left. And Don Anderson isn't in very good shape. So pretty quick there won't be anyone who knew him.

James Plath

144

TILLIE ARNOLD:
Sun Valley Years

Tillie Arnold's husband, Lloyd R. "Pappy" Arnold, published *High on the Wild* in 1969 (Caxton Printers), a pictorial recollection of Ernest Hemingway's years in Idaho. After his retirement in 1962, Arnold spent seven years assembling material for the book as a memorial to the man he loved. Arnold was on assignment to photograph Sun Valley, then in its early stages of development, and that assignment extended into twenty years. Averell Harriman and the Union Pacific Railroad had conceived of Sun Valley as a skiing mecca, and later Sun Valley became a year-round western playground. In these early years, Hemingway, by his own admission, was a tourist attraction, a publicity property hired to work and play in Sun Valley with full run of the fishing and hunting in the Sawtooth and Pioneer Mountains which surrounded the complex. Tillie, of course, accompanied her husband, who accompanied Hemingway—whether it was a gathering for hunting trips, bird shooting, picnicking, or simply dinner and drinks. Today, Tillie survives her husband and is in retirement in Buhl, Idaho. The interview took place on September 29, 1998.

Frank Simons: I'm reminded of the wonderful photo taken of you sitting with Hemingway in his Buick convertible.

Tillie Arnold: Yes, and that photo wasn't a planned thing. He had a new car and the man standing with us is Toby Bruce, his man Friday, who had driven Papa and Marty to Sun Valley. This was in 1939. Toby had gotten out of the car and my husband was taking pictures. I just happened to be there and someone suggested I get in the car with Papa. That was a very long time ago. Pappy died in 1970, and I've been alone for quite awhile.

FS: Do you recall your first meeting with Hemingway?

TA: Yes, the day after he arrived in Sun Valley. He told me I looked like Pauline, his second wife. Pappy, my husband, and I met him in the Challenger Inn. It was about nine o'clock when we walked in as they were having breakfast. He had asked Lloyd the day before if he was married, and Lloyd said "yes," and he said, "Well, why don't you join us in the morning, and bring your wife?" So we went in and I happened to be dressed in western clothes. He suddenly stopped laughing and smiling altogether, and when we walked across the dining room he never took his eyes off me. He was actually staring at me, and I thought, What in the heck? I wondered, What's wrong? Then he began saying a lot of things to Marty [Gellhorn] and they began laughing again. Marty apologized and then Papa explained that I had "spooked" him—that I had spooked the hell out of him. He said that I looked like Pauline—close enough to be her sister. I had seen pictures of her, but I didn't think there was much resemblance at all. But he said that my coloring and round cheeks—round much like his own, he added—reminded him of her, and he wasn't expecting to see Pauline in Idaho. You see, the divorce was not yet final.

Anyway, he hoped I wasn't offended, and of course I wasn't. He wanted to know how I'd come to have the name "Tillie," and was it short for Mathilda? Yes, I told him, and I explained that in the twenties, when the young ladies began frequenting barber shops and had their hair shingled very short in back, that my father said I looked like Tillie the Toiler, and the name "Tillie" stuck. Papa continued discussing the resemblance [to Pauline] and said that if I had tan saddle pants, shirt and chamois jacket with a wide-brimmed hat, he could imagine my standing in a safari tent. He said, "If you'd had a hat on, I would have thought she was tailing me!" I laughed and said, "Do you mean P.O.M.?" And he actually blushed. Later, he said to Gregory and Patrick, when they came in 1940 and first saw me, "Who do you think this lady looks like?" And they said, "Our mother."

Anyway, when we sat down at the table, as the maitre d' pushed the chair in for me, I sat there for a few minutes and thought, What a breakfast! Finally, I just couldn't contain myself. I said to him, "Mr. Hemingway, is that breakfast? And he said, "Yes, have some, Daughter. It's good for the kidneys." He had a plate of marinated herring and two steins of beer, one half full. I thought that was very funny, and he laughed too. From that time on, we were the best of friends. I was always very comfortable whenever I was with Papa. I think he was the best friend I ever had, from the moment of our first

At Sun Valley: Otto "Toby" Bruce, Tillie Arnold, Hemingway, 1940.

Photograph by Lloyd Arnold, courtesy of John F. Kennedy Library

meeting. We had many good times together.

FS: Did you confide in one another?

TA: Yes, we did, though he never discussed his work too much with anyone. Once in awhile we talked of concerns we had. When Marty was gone to Finland and he was alone, we were together a lot because he was new at Sun Valley. As he was writing *For Whom the Bell Tolls,* he asked us if we'd care to read the work-in-progress, which Pappy and I both did. I recall now that many years later, in the fifties, he would tell me of how he couldn't write anymore and that nothing sounded right when he got it down.

So yes, I think we were very close. After that, when we were off hunting someplace, I started calling him "Papa." I didn't call him Papa that first year until after the boys had been there and called him Papa. It just became sort of normal for me to call him Papa as

147

well. I think I may have started the notion of calling him Papa—at least at Sun Valley. Eventually, practically everyone was calling him Papa.

FS: Did he speak of any difficulty with Marty?

TA: She was wonderful. I liked her very much. I never heard a cross word between them—no arguments or anything like that. Never. But it was during the war and they weren't married yet. They went to the Burma Road together. Papa didn't want her to go alone, and told her that he'd rather she didn't go, because it was a rough trip. But she insisted, and she finally got the assignment for *Collier's*. There had been another lady who had the assignment, but had decided against it because of the difficulty of it. So Marty got it. And I said to her, "Marty, I think you're crazy to go on a trip like that and leave your new man. I just think that's bad." And she said, "Tillie, I'd rather have that assignment than anything else in the world." She said, "I guess it's just in my blood. I can't help it." So Papa went with her—he got a news assignment too—and they agreed when they got the divorce that she wouldn't write anything that would mention his name at all, so she didn't. When she wrote of being over there long after that, she called him "Unwilling Companion," but with just the initials U.C. And she referred to him all through the story as U.C. But when she got back, she admitted that she would never have been able to make the trip without Ernest. She always called him Ernest.

FS: Hemingway did a great deal of hunting and fishing in the Sun Valley area. Did you hunt with him very often?

TA: Oh, yes. I didn't get to go all the time, but when there were women in the hunting party, Papa always took care to see that we were given a good position so that we'd have good shooting. But if I didn't go, I would always see them when they got back and we would get together for drinks. When we were in his suite the second evening—he invited us over to room 208—he said that Mr. Rogers had put him in a pretty fancy wigwam. I said, "Yes, there have been a lot of very important people who have stayed in this suite." "Oh?" he said. "We'll have to call it Glamour House." And it was called Glamour House from then on.

FS: Do you recall your thoughts of when you learned that Hemingway had shot himself?

TA: Well, I knew that he would do it. I just had a feeling that he would. Of course, he had tried several times before. He had the guns and the ammunition and everything. Even so, I felt that it should never have happened, because I think Mary should have gotten the guns out of the house. I asked her, "As long as you locked the ammunition up, why don't you lock the guns up?" And she said, "Well, that's the first thing that Papa would look for when he would get home from Rochester." I guess she didn't feel that it was necessary as long as the ammunition was locked up.

FS: Had you talked to him when he wasn't feeling well?

TA: Yes. He came to me for many things to chat about, and to complain to me about.

FS: Can you recall his complaints?

TA: He complained about going to Rochester, that he didn't want to go there anymore. He had this idea that he had an incurable disease and that nothing could be done about it. He had said, as far back as 1939, that he was mad at his father for committing suicide. He thought he was a coward for taking his own life. He said there are only three reasons for killing yourself. If you had an incurable disease, that was one. Or if you were tortured beyond endurance, like if you were a prisoner of war. And the third acceptable reason was if you are hastening a drowning because you can't swim all of the sea. But then he said, "If you don't live behind the eyes, you can't expect to see all of the view."

FS: Did you know Mary well?

TA: I knew Mary extremely well. We all called her "Miss Mary." I remember, he used to complain to me about Mary, and I would say, "Oh, Papa, Mary loves you and wouldn't do anything against you"— you know, little things that would bother him about her. I always took her part, but later I thought that maybe it was the wrong thing for me to have said, because he needed help. He couldn't write anymore. After those terrible shock treatments he said, "I can't write anymore. They fooled with my think-machine." And it wasn't too long after that that I was attending his funeral. It was a private funeral, an outdoor service. People had to have a card to attend. The priest didn't know him and wasn't very specific during the eulogy, so maybe that's the reason I can't remember anything about what he said. I was very upset at the funeral, thinking about the things Papa had told me. And I sure did miss him when he was gone. We were so close. He had called me Daughter for a long time.

FS: Did you visit him at the Finca?

TA: No, we didn't get down there. We were invited to go down, but we just couldn't seem to get away. We had our father and mother with us, and Father was ill about two years and then he died. We had a house in Ketchum, and Mother lived with us for about eleven years.

FS: What about good times? Shooting parties, for example, that you were part of?

TA: They used to shoot clay pigeons in back, where the drive came in. There were no houses or buildings close, so they shot a lot of trap there. There would be four or five of them shooting, and they used to have a thing where if you hit the bird you'd get a drink from the bottle, but if you missed you stayed dry. Papa, of course, was an excellent shot and got more than his share of the bottle.

FS: Was caution a concern during hunts?

TA: They were experts with their guns. Wherever you hunted, you didn't have any liquor. After the hunt they could have a drink or two, but not during the hunting. The guns had to be put away first.

FS: Who was running the show?

TA: Papa was the general. Everyone looked to him for direction. The first year he came was the first hunting season open at Sun Valley, because they only intended in the beginning when the lodge was built that it would be just a ski resort. Then they decided it would be a year-round resort and put up more buildings. When they put Papa in the lodge, they had told him that they had closed skiing just a week before and would he mind going to the Challenger Inn or The Ram for meals. They served lunch in The Ram, which Papa was especially fond of. They had a nice bar and good food. He enjoyed that very much. Music, dancing.

FS: And other celebrities?

TA: Gary Cooper came in 1940. He had been invited, along with Papa, the year before, but he was making a film and said he would make it the next year, which he did, and practically every other year that Papa was there, and sometimes when Papa wasn't there. But Papa never did meet Clark Gable because they were never there at the same time. He knew Ingrid Bergman and was very fond of her.

Hunting in Idaho, 1941: Gregory, Jack, Ernest, Martha, Patrick.

FS: What can you recall that might be typical of his stay at Sun Valley?

TA: He loved picnics. Lloyd would go into the kitchen and they would pack the lunch and it would be wonderful. About five of us would pack it up and run over to Silver Creek, or somewhere like that. Sometimes, if they were here, the [Hemingway] boys would go with us.

FS: Did he relate to his children well?

TA: I thought he did. It's been said that he wasn't a good father. If he was writing, he would often complain that they were making too much noise, or something like that. That's what I've been told, but I never knew him anyplace but here at Sun Valley or in Ketchum. He was a very congenial, happy person. But when he came back in 1958, we knew that Papa was a sick man.

There was a little incident when Mary wrote and wanted Lloyd to find a place for them to stay. Lloyd was always making some crazy crack about something, and I don't know, he made some remark which I don't recall now, but it bothered Papa. And he wrote and said that if Lloyd felt that way, maybe he wasn't wanted, or if Lloyd had a problem with their coming he should just say so. He said, "Don't hesitate to say if you think there is a reason that I shouldn't come, because if anyone would write to me now and want me to come down and go out on the water, it isn't the same as it was, and fishing has not been good at all. I would tell them not to come, because it just isn't good right now."

Lloyd said to me that there was something wrong with the tone of the letter, that Papa is not a well man. I agreed, because he had never been so pessimistic before. So Lloyd got right on the phone and called Toby Bruce and told him to get in touch with Papa and tell him to get the hell out here. And then he wrote another letter, and that was it. He was happy as could be about coming back. But we knew. We could see certain little signs that he wasn't like he was before. He hadn't been here for ten years. He then came in '58, '59, and '60. On the thirtieth of June they got to Ketchum in the afternoon to the house that he had bought in the interim. George Brown had driven them. George Brown had a professional boxing ring in New York where they would work out. When Papa would go to New York, he would always see George, a very old friend, and they would box. Papa had asked Mary to get in touch with George and ask him if he would drive him back from Rochester, which George did. So this was on the thirtieth of June and he was in Ketchum on the first day of July and he shot himself on the second. That was the only time he'd been here in the summer. I always thought that if he had spent some summers here, he would have loved them. But anyway, George was with Mary when it happened.

Did you by chance see his biography [A&E, 1998] on television a few nights ago? I thought it was wonderful, and his granddaughter [Mariel] did such a great job. You know, she never knew her grandfather. Her mother was pregnant with her when Papa died. But she certainly had a lot of good information. I miss Papa. And of course I miss my husband. I never remarried, and we were ten days short of being married for forty-two years.

FS: Do you reflect on those years in Sun Valley and Ketchum?

TA: I had wonderful times with Papa. He was always very kind and nice to me, and he was a real gentleman. I think he was hard on Mary, and I don't know why, and I don't know what happened for sure. Dr. George Saviers would take Papa's blood pressure every day, practically, because it was so high the last couple of years. But then he hadn't met Papa before the Sun Valley years. George, of course, had been in the service, and after his discharge was off to become a doctor.

I remember once when Papa had tried to jump over a fence like some of the other boys did, and he sprained an ankle [laughs]. It wasn't a bad sprain, but enough to bother him for maybe a week. Papa was very fond of George, who took good care of him.

FS: Did you appreciate Hemingway's sense of humor?

TA: Of course. I remember he accused Lloyd of robbing the cradle. Lloyd said, "No I didn't. She's the same age as Gene Van Guilder [Lloyd's friend]," and at that time I was thirty-four. But I did look young for my age, and I wish I did now [laughs] at ninety-three. But I was looking at the pictures for quite awhile after Lloyd was gone, and they brought back so many memories and conversations that I thought, Tillie—in fact, I said it out loud—"Tillie, you really led a more than interesting life, and you really didn't know it!" I met so many interesting people, knowing Gary Cooper and Clark Gable quite well, for example. But of all of them I thought Papa the most interesting. He was a person that a lot of people said was blustery or belligerent, but it was impossible for us to imagine that. Cuba or Key West, those settings are pretty rough, but not here in Ketchum. And there are those who said he was a drunk. I don't know of anyone who saw him drunk. He could drink a lot, mind you—especially wine, having learned to do it in Paris in the earlier years—but you could never tell if he'd been drinking. When I think about it all now, as late as 1959, when he was so troubled and worried so much about his own finances, he'd say to me, "How're you fixed for dough?" and "Are you sure?" He thought he was broke, but would still offer money. He was so kind to us, and it was so wonderful to have spent those good years with him.

Frank Simons

Christmas, 1959. Papa, Tillie Arnold, Miss Mary, Lloyd "Pappy" Arnold, Pete and Dot Hill.
"Papa was harassing me as I took the picture." - F. MacMullen

154

WILLIAM W. SEWARD:
An Epistolary Friendship

William W. Seward chaired the English Department at Old Dominion University for many years and had a friendship with Ernest Hemingway which spanned two decades. Most of their correspondence was by letter, but occasionally they were able to match their busy schedules so that they were able to get together. After Hemingway's death, Seward published his book, *My Friend, Ernest Hemingway* [Barnes, 1969]. Now, less than a year from the centennial of Hemingway's birth, Professor Seward resides in Virginia Beach, Virginia, and in retirement spends the winter months with his wife and family at Sand Key, off Clearwater Beach, Florida. The interview took place September 8, 1998.

Frank Simons: What was the inspiration for the writing of your book, *My Friend, Ernest Hemingway*?

William Seward: When Hemingway was alive, I had never thought to write a book about him, but after he died and I began reading all of these articles and books that came out, I decided that I needed to write something. So, I published the book, *My Friend, Ernest Hemingway*, in 1969. I had finished it around 1966, and the version that I had at the time was a standard-length book, not a long book, but between 250-300 pages. But it was just another book on Hemingway, and I wasn't satisfied. I didn't know what to do, so I just put it aside. In the summer of '67, I took my family to Europe, and we stayed over almost three months. It was a rather strange thing that while I was in a hotel in Rome, it just struck me like a bolt of lightning that I had to shorten it and make every word count and have nothing in there that had been in print before. I decided, as a result, that it had to be a short book. I had been thumbing through my library before I'd gone to Europe, and I'd run across this book by Tom Wicker, the journalist, called *Kennedy Without Tears*. It was a fine book, and it was only about forty-some pages long, but actually was on the best-seller list for a long time. Anyhow, that gave me the spark. As soon as I got home that fall, I started rewriting, and came up with the book, *My Friend,* which was a little under 100 pages. Fortunately, it was very well reviewed.

FS: As the title implies, your book is a memoir of your friendship as opposed to biography?

WS: Yes. My hope was to dispel in some way a misinterpretation of the man—to counteract some of the biographers and critics who had written perhaps out of envy, and in some cases, in very bad taste, as well as those who promoted questionable details that read more like sensational gossip. Yet, as discriminating as I was with the book, I think the legend, unfortunately as legends always do, will continue to beat the truth in the end. Even so, I tried to adhere to the obligations of a trusted friend in presenting his conversations.

FS: Had you been writing to him for some time?

WS: Yes, I had. In fact, I had corresponded with him more than I saw him. Although I did not see much of Ernest personally, we maintained a twenty-year, informal correspondence.

FS: You believe, then, that you were able to know the man, although you met with him only occasionally?

WS: In some ways, the friendly correspondence such as we had can be more revealing than constant in-the-flesh association. Ernest himself once remarked that "You write a friend and have much the same contact as though you were together. You exchange letters and it is almost as good as talking."

FS: Nevertheless, would you have preferred to see him more often?

WS: Of course. But for one thing, it got so that few of his friends saw him much after the war, because he was always gone. Either he was in Africa, Spain, or France, or somewhere. Despite what his so-called friends may say, it was impossible for them to be with him for what I would call a great deal of time.

FS: Did you base your book on this correspondence?

WS: Yes, and I had to either paraphrase the letters or else take the idea and put it in my own words, because that was long before Baker's *Selected Letters* was published. Hemingway had this edict that he did not want any of his personal letters published.

FS: Of course, that didn't come to pass.

WS: No, that part of his will was not honored, but I had no wish to violate a friendship. And I know that had he been living, he would have prompted me not to publish our letters.

There is one letter of mine in Baker's collection. Carlos told me that the reason for there being only one letter was that he tried not to have any repetition, and that he chose the letters on the basis of their content, that, on the whole, the other letters did not have. I noticed there was but one letter to Faulkner, although I know that they were not close friends. So it's there, and it was written in the spring of 1947. In the letter to me he wrote of his son, Patrick, who was suffering from a concussion he'd gotten in an automobile accident, and various other illnesses in the family which had put him behind schedule with his new novel, *Across the River and Into the Trees*. He'd taken time from caring for Patrick to write to me, and indicated that he was pleased that I was teaching *Crime and Punishment* at the time. He had a great admiration for the Russian novelist [Fyodor Dostoevsky], and suggested I might also consider teaching *The Brothers Karamazov* or *The Gambler*.

FS: Other than your own book, do you have a preference for another Hemingway biography?

WS: Well, Baker's, I believe, remains for me the most definitive. But there have been others I admire, including Scott Donaldson's, who taught at William and Mary. After Denis Brian's interviews began appearing in *The Atlantic Monthly*, Donaldson called me and had me speak at his graduate seminars. So I was a friend of his, and I may be a bit prejudiced, but his is a well-written book—and unlike some psychological interpretations, very sound.

FS: What compelled you to write your first letter to Hemingway?

WS: I wrote to him first in March of 1940. I expressed an admiration, a high respect for his writing, because some of it I had used in the classroom. And his reply was a fine letter, and he mentioned in the letter that he was finishing a novel, which, of course, was *For Whom the Bell Tolls*. It was coming out that fall, and he thought it was the best thing that he had done, and that he wanted to send me a copy. I thought, having known a number of authors, that in the intervening months he would have forgotten. Plus the fact that I was teaching at the University of Richmond at the time, and I'd received a teaching fellowship at Duke, and so I went to Duke that fall to begin my doctorate. So, I sent him a note that I'd not be at Richmond, but at the address in Durham. Lo and behold, not too long after that, the signed copy of *For Whom the Bell Tolls* came in, and he had written my name along with "wishing him all good luck, always."

FS: So that was the beginning of a pleasant correspondence?

WS: Very pleasant, although I don't think it was planned. We simply continued to write to each other. I say this very modestly, but we seemed to have established a rapport. I think he got the idea that I wasn't trying to capitalize on him, and, of course, I wasn't. As it turned out, we came to be very good friends.

FS: Having taught Hemingway for many years, which of his works do you find most significant?

WS: I think *For Whom the Bell Tolls* is his best work. I realize there are many who don't agree, but Hemingway thought so. He never changed his mind. He told me at the time, before it came out, that he considered that it would be his best novel. To my knowledge, he never changed that view. Of course, it's a view that may be unpopular with some scholars, but generally, I still think it's his best book. I don't believe this is true because of the political crisis in Spain, necessarily, because he was never interested in politics in the narrow sense of the word. The book was of epic proportion much more so than his previous novels. All of the characters were identifiable to the reader in the tragic sense, but particularly Robert Jordan and Maria. His sympathies were with the little people, and this novel, as much as *A Farewell to Arms,* for example, and then finally with *The Old Man and the Sea,* identifies with everyman's struggle.

FS: Did Hemingway mention projects that he may have been working on?

WS: Oh, yes. He mentioned them from time to time, but he did not like to talk much of anything that was a work in progress. He did write a number of letters during the composition of *Across the River and Into the Trees*. He knew that I was going to review it professionally. In fact, I guess I told him, and he was very pleased with the review, and after the review came out in the *Virginia Pilot,* he told me that next to the *London Times,* he thought it was the best review of the book that he'd seen.

FS: *Across the River and Into the Trees* did not receive many favorable reviews.

WS: I guess I knew, from what he had told me, a little more of

Mary Hemingway, William W. Seward, and Ernest Hemingway.
October, 1957.

what he was trying to do. And I still think, although it is not a major novel, that it is a better book than the reviews generally stated. I believe the book to be much more complex than it appears to be. The complexity of it was not noted. I remember in one letter he had mentioned that he knew that I was going to review it, and he said, "You can damn it to hell and still be my good friend."

FS: Can you speak more specifically of the novel's complexity?

WS: I believe that *Across the River and Into the Trees* was an effort by Hemingway to experiment. I think, contrary to what William Faulkner once said, that he had the courage to go in other directions, and that it was an important part of his development as a writer. The tone, the language, that eventually evolved into *The Old Man and the Sea,* can be detected in *Across the River and Into the Trees.* I believe his style was shifting in another direction and that it was a conscious consideration on his part. I know from our conversations that he had a very high regard for *Across the River.* I think the book reflects courage, and I found it to be much more poetic than his previous work. Perhaps that may account for its poor reception with most of his critics. Nor were they accustomed to the tone of the novel. It's not possible to overstate the note of sadness. They are the tired cadences of the direct speech of a man's heart who is expressing that emotion for the first time. Whether he's speaking of hunting, fishing, sexual intercourse, or the correlating emotions of sorrow, pain, and death, this emotional accuracy is the major reason for the haunting tone which he consistently maintains throughout the novel. After all, though I still believe the book not his best, he definitely made efforts to do new things—and oftentimes, as with anyone, experimentation falls short.

FS: Had he mentioned any other work in progress?

WS: Yes, when he was writing *The Old Man and the Sea,* of which he'd mentioned that he was going to send a copy. As it turned out, he was in Mombasa when the book came out, but he had sent an inscribed card to Scribner's and had them put it in the book and send it on to me. Of course, I was very proud of it. It was thoughtful and very generous of him, I thought. He had a reputation of not approving of professors who were interested in his work. In fact, Mary once told me that, as far as she knew, "You are the only university person that he was ever close to."

FS: Had he ever discussed with you works in progress that were published posthumously?

WS: After I had expressed interest in a number of stories to be published in *The Atlantic Monthly,* he mentioned that his next book was to be a book of short stories. He said he had almost enough stories and that it was to be about Africa, but that he had to go back to make sure of a few details.

FS: Was it your understanding that this book was to be based on his second safari with Mary?

WS: Yes, I'm quite sure it must have been. It could well be the book that Scribner's announced several weeks ago, *True at First Light,* which his son Patrick edited for publication next spring for the centennial.

FS: And it was your understanding that Hemingway intended it to be a collection of short stories, rather than a novel?

WS: Oh, yes. He spoke of it as "a book of stories."

FS: How do you feel about the publication of posthumous work?

WS: I've not been happy with it, because Hemingway is not editing the work and someone else is making decisions as to what must be cut and what stays. Consequently, there is a great danger in misinterpreting what the author intended, which is what I believe happened to *The Garden of Eden*. I didn't like the book at all, as I said, because it didn't seem to fit together. And now Scribner's announcement that *True at First Light* was to be a novel, yet the author had mentioned to me that it was a collection of stories.

FS: There is a fine tribute to you in Mary Hemingway's book, *How It Was*. She writes that a "young professor of English from Norfolk, Virginia, William W. Seward, Jr., who for several years had been letter-writing with Ernest, joined us at the railway station to ride back with us to Norfolk. After Mr. Seward had left us, Ernest declared, 'Bill's a fine-textured guy. A legitimate gent.'"

WS: Yes, and I very much appreciated the compliment. As I said, because Hemingway was away, opportunities to actually meet with him were rare. We had an open invitation to visit him in Cuba, but with his schedule and my university schedule it was next to impossible to arrange visits. Plus, a lot of times he didn't know in advance where he was going to be. Usually, I saw him in New York, where he and Mary had an apartment which she continued to maintain after his death for many years—at least up until she became very ill herself.

But I recall joining them at the railway station. This was the trip that I'd come down to meet him when he was on his way to Miami, in October of 1957. He had called me. He was in the States, which I knew, because there had been something in the columns about his attending the championship prize fight in which Sugar Ray Robinson was defending his title against Carmen Basilio. And since the World Series was in New York that fall, he'd also attended a few games. But I didn't know that I was going to see him on that trip, plus, knowing his aversion to using the telephone, I was surprised when he called me on a Thursday, October 3rd, and said that he would be coming through. Mary was spending Friday night in Washington with some friends, and she was going to meet him at the train. He wanted me to ride down, which I did. I flew up to Washington and met Ernest and Mary at Union Station and got on the train with them. They were with Denis Zaphiro, who was a game warden in Kenya at the time. Zaphiro had befriended the Hemingways while they were on their safari of 1953. He was a young Englishman who had joined Ernest and Mary in New York. Ernest told me that Denis had never been down the East Coast, and so they decided to take the train trip so he could see a fairly decent slice of the coast. So that's how Zaphiro fit into the picture.

FS: On these occasions, what do you recall of Hemingway's personality. Was it what you'd expected?

WS: I know that many thought Hemingway to be aloof—perhaps mean-spirited. But these impressions did not reflect anything of the man I knew. Many, unfortunately, had mistakenly taken some interviews literally, such as the Lillian Ross interview. But to my mind, he was just putting on a good act, because I never saw any of this when I was with them. He was always very cordial with me, and I experienced none of that sort of thing. When I talk about him, reflect upon our friendship, a passage of Ezra Pound's comes to mind. Pound said that "I always saw Ernest at his best." And that was the case with me, although I'm sure that there are people who probably have good reason to have a negative reaction to him. In that regard, I have to disqualify myself and say that my experience was the same as Ezra Pound's. I always saw him at his best.

I was also impressed, as I know most people were, with his physical presence. I'm six feet tall, and I had to look up to him. I would guess he was six-two, at least. He was stocky, imposing because of his heavy shoulders and deep chest, even though the last time I saw him in '57, he'd lost some weight and was down to about 200 pounds. He'd lost about 25 pounds, but he still had a special presence about him. He was apparently in pretty good health. There had been a lot in newspaper columns about his health at the time, particularly about his blood pressure, which he had gotten under control. The doctors had taken him off whiskey. However, when we got in his drawing room on the train, he brought out all these bottles and wanted to know what I drank. Occasionally I would drink socially in those days. I was surprised when he asked me to join them in a drink. Later he told me that while he had only cut down on alcohol, he had lost the necessary weight. He had opened a large leather bag sitting in their drawing room. It was well-stocked with a large assortment of whiskey bottles. Mary smiled and said, "For writers we drink very little, you know."

Mary had a martini, Ernest had his usual scotch, and I took bourbon. At one point, among a number of toasts, he said, "Bill

Seward is my loyal friend who never lets me down, and whenever everybody else says Dr. Hemingstein is on the skids, Bill Seward sticks by me." We drank fairly steadily on down the coast. He was the sort, despite what a lot of people have said about him, who could drink quite a bit, and you'd never know it. I'm sure there were times when people could tell he'd been drinking, but ordinarily, when he would sit, and just in a friendly way, sip away, at least I could never tell that he'd had a drink. So we had a fine time. There was some talk of art and baseball. Then someone brought up the flight of the first Russian Sputnik which had gone into orbit the day before. He laughed at the talk he'd heard in New York the night before and mimicked, "Let's make peace now! Let's make peace!" But then he became very serious about the subject, knowing full-well the technological import of it. Later, as we traveled down the coast, past the marine base at Quantico, and then on down past the battlefields outside Fredericksburg, we had quite a serious discussion about war. I found it informative because here was a man who had participated in five wars, either as a combatant or correspondent. After some discussion, he closed the topic with, "Never think that war, no matter how necessary, nor how justified, is not a crime."

There are plenty of people who are sort of anti-Hemingway—in fact, they may be in the majority. A colleague of mine said to me more than once, "Bill, I think he had a mean streak." And I said, "Well, maybe he did, but I never saw it. If you take people in general, and you were with them all the time, you'd find that most people have a mean streak at one time or another." But that side never came out with me.

I remember one time that we were kidding and I said, "You know, you lived in Florida for a number of years, so maybe the critics ought to list you as a Southern writer. And he chuckled and laughed and said, "Well, that makes more sense than a lot of things they say about me." He had a marvelous sense of humor. He once spoke of an occasion when some acquaintance reprimanded him for not going to somebody's funeral, somebody he knew, and Ernest said, "A son-of-a-bitch alive is a son-of-a-bitch dead!" [laughs]. Frankly, there's some truth to that.

FS: So you would, from time to time, meet with Mary and Hemingway in New York?

WS: Yes, we visited them in their apartment, and after his death, Mary used to visit us in Norfolk. I had a sort of standing invitation, and was to let them know whenever I was going to be in New York when they were there, which, quite frankly, was not often. But, usually, it was not a formal invitation. If I knew he was going to be there and I could get there myself, I would let him know by calling him.

FS: Were you fond of Mary as well?

WS: Yes, and when Hemingway was alive, Mary was a bouncer—she tried to keep people away from him—and she was much more formal. But after he died, she loosened up, and, as I said, we used to visit, and visited almost right up to the time of her last illness. I knew her quite well.

FS: Were you familiar with her concerns about biographies of Hemingway?

WS: I know that she'd reached a point that she detested Hotchner because of his *Papa* book. She was very opposed to its publication, and tried to get an injunction to prevent its release. She became, I would say, an enemy of Hotchner's. As a matter of fact, she was not all that pleased with Baker's book. I remember when she was visiting with us, well along during the composition of Baker's *Ernest Hemingway: A Life Story,* she was very displeased and said, "How would you like to take it over?" I'm sure she was just making conversation, but her point was that she was not happy with it. She got to the point that she would continue to recount how many mistakes and factual errors that she was finding in a certain number of pages in Carlos's book. She then would mention the accuracy of my book. I like to believe that she wasn't patronizing me, because she also made reference to the accuracy of my book in her endorsement on the dust jacket.

FS: Did Mary speak of why she finally gave permission to Baker for the publication of Hemingway's letters, even though Hemingway specifically directed that they not be published after his death?

WS: I never discussed that with her. Neither of us ever brought it up. I have no specific idea what brought that about.

FS: What would your feeling be about it?

WS: I'd hate to say, except that in life, all so often, things get down to money. I have no real idea whether that was part of it, because I don't think Mary was a particularly mercenary person. I knew Carlos, and I felt it was a worthwhile project. Since he'd not been allowed to publish excerpts of letters in the biography, he decided that he'd like to come out with *Selected Letters*. Of course, she had to agree, but what that story is about is her decision, and I don't know. In any case, the publishing of the letters is of great value to the literary world. Hemingway, despite all the bluster, was a very private person. While he didn't want his personal words made public, nevertheless, the book is a great contribution.

FS: What do you think of Mary's decision to publish posthumous work?

WS: Well, that has puzzled me. *Islands in the Stream,* of course, but even more puzzling, *The Garden of Eden.*

FS: Could you elaborate?

WS: With *The Garden of Eden,* perhaps it's because the book was garbled so from the manuscript—and of course he didn't have it in any condition for its being publishable—but it has always saddened me that the book was published. I don't think that somebody, even someone your own age, could take a manuscript and bring it about the way you intended it to be. And I think the chap who was given that responsibility was just a young fellow, not more than his early thirties, at that. It's an interesting book and appears to be basically well-written, but as a novel, it doesn't fit together as I thought it should. I also thought it an obvious departure from his writing style, certainly more so than *Islands in the Stream.* It just didn't sound like Hemingway.

FS: Did you find it unusual that Mary was the sole beneficiary of his estate, thereby excluding his sons?

WS: I am familiar with the will, which, of course, was made public. It appeared as if Hemingway had drawn it up himself, or, at any rate, it was obvious that it had not been written by a trained legal person—that is, a lawyer who might specialize in wills. As you know, he had indicated that he trusted Mary to take care of everything, and that she would see that the boys were taken care of. I didn't have much reaction to it. But I have two daughters and two grandchildren. So it seems strange to me, but then I'm sure that their family life is not like mine, because I live one block from my older

165

daughter, and within three minutes of my younger—almost like they were still kids, with the grandchildren here almost as much as they are home. It seems, however, very strange that his sons were left out of his will. Maybe his gradual decline in the last years contributed to his decision, plus the fact that he didn't see his children as often as we might see ours, and though he sometimes took his children with him, out west or to Cuba, much of the time they were apart.

FS: Hemingway's sons, John, Patrick, and Gregory, have spoken of Hemingway as a good father.

WS: Yes, and that includes Gregory. Of the three, I would expect him to have less close feeling for his father than the other two.

FS: Why would you say that?

WS: Well, it's public knowledge that Gregory had some difficult times with his father and he says as much in his book, but for the most part, the book was complimentary of his father.

FS: As a Hemingway scholar, do you feel Hemingway's work will continue to endure beyond the nineties?

WS: I think that Hemingway's fiction is just as relevant today as when he was alive and writing. His works are replete with universal themes of loyalty, honesty, and courage, to mention a few. Plus the fact that he did so much for the evolution of the language—perhaps more than professional critics realize—and therefore has revolutionized the written language. Granted, he has sometimes been considered politically incorrect, and, for some, perhaps, remains as such today. But I believe that there is no question that his literary influence will remain with us.

FS: How late in Hemingway's life were you still writing to one another?

WS: The last letter that I received from him was mailed from Rochester's Mayo Clinic, and it was during the spring, within months of his death on July 2, so it was probably in April, several months earlier. He was hospitalized at the time that he wrote it, and as far as I remember, it is the only letter that I ever received from him that was dictated. It was a typed letter that he was not able to type himself, evidently, but he did sign it himself. It was an unusual letter, and yet, it was sort of typical of his relationship with me because in the first letter he'd offered to send the novel, which he

166

did. In this last letter, he said that when he got home, if the season was right, he would like to send us a brace of ducks on ice, which he was not able to do. When he got home, evidently he could hardly function, and was not doing well at all. Anyway, that was the last of a series of letters which were not necessarily on a periodic basis, but again, much of the time, he was off traveling—Africa, Asia, and, of course, Europe. I would say there were probably twenty-five to thirty letters that spanned a good twenty years.

FS: Could you describe your reaction when you heard he'd died?

WS: I was terribly shocked. In late June of that year Mary sent an unexpected message that Ernest's health was improving. About two weeks later we had just returned home from a trip, and as I walked in the house the phone was ringing. I thought, how typical to hear the phone ring after returning from vacation and getting back to the routine. But it was my nephew, who had been a Hemingway fan since his late teens. He said, "Bill, have you heard the news?" And then he told me that Ernest Hemingway had shot himself early that morning. I remember hoping that maybe this was another episode from his seemingly charmed life, and that he would emerge from it as before, battered, perhaps, but intact.

The newscasters' reports did not hit me deeply at first. It took awhile for that to happen. I believe his physical condition was the thing that brought him down, moreso than his mind. I realize that he was suffering from a mental condition, but, as I said, I had received a letter from him at the time, and he sounded fairly normal. I believe his death had more to do with the depletion of his physical health. And he just couldn't take it anymore.

Frank Simons

Photograph by Zarina Mullan Plath

James Plath is a Hemingway scholar who ran with the bulls in Pamplona and directed the Hemingway Days Writers' Workshop & Conference in Key West for ten years. A professor of English at Illinois Wesleyan University, he has also published on John Updike and Raymond Carver, and, as editor of *Clockwatch Review (a journal of the arts)* he has interviewed such creative talents as Jimmy Buffett, Dawn Upshaw, Romare Bearden, Buddy Guy, Vincent Price, and Arlo Guthrie.

Photograph by Nancy Newman

Frank Simons completed his Hemingway graduate research at the University of Wisconsin. He presently teaches American literature and creative writing at Sarasota (Florida) High School. Mr. Simons has a novel in progress on the Klondike Gold Rush, is the author of poetry and short stories, and is involved in a pilot program that measures student curriculum mastery via computers. Any free time is spent fly fishing for North Carolina, Hiwassee River rainbow/brown trout.

This first edition of 2,000 hardcover and 6,500 softcover books, includes two hundred copies numbered and signed by the authors to commemorate the one hundredth anniversary of Ernest Hemingway's birth.

———